THE
POWER
OF POSITIVE
WORDS

STAN TOLER

HARVEST HOUSE PUBLISHERS
EUGENE, OREGON

Cover by Bryce Williamson

Cover photo © Creative-Touch / Getty Images

The Power of Positive Words

Copyright © 2019 Stan Toler
Published by Harvest House Publishers
Eugene, Oregon 97408
www.harvesthousepublishers.com

ISBN 978-0-7369-7500-1 (pbk.)
ISBN 978-0-7369-7501-8 (eBook)

Library of Congress Cataloging-in-Publication Data

Names: Toler, Stan, author.
Title: The power of positive words / Stan Toler.
Description: Eugene : Harvest House Publishers, 2018. | Includes
  bibliographical references.
Identifiers: LCCN 2018030159 (print) | LCCN 2018046466 (ebook) | ISBN
  9780736975018 (ebook) | ISBN 9780736975001 (pbk.)
Subjects: LCSH: Language and languages--Religious aspects--Christianity. |
  Vocabulary.
Classification: LCC BR115.L25 (ebook) | LCC BR115.L25 T65 2018 (print) | DDC
  241/.672--dc23
LC record available at https://lccn.loc.gov/2018030159

Printed in the United States of America

19 20 21 22 23 24 25 26 27 / BP-SK / 10 9 8 7 6 5

CONTENTS

THE POWER OF YOUR WORDS SHAPES YOUR OUTCOMES

Throughout the course of time, words have shaped and impacted various outcomes. The number of significant words and phrases quoted from world-changers are in many ways historical anchors for what we say and who we have become as individuals, our culture, and as a nation. Words form powerful statements and become memorable markers of our culture.

And with the influence of media and social media, our words carry a much greater influence on how words are leveraged, used, and shape our culture—both positively and negatively.

Leaders desire positive outcomes, but many are unaware of how their thoughts and words may undermine their success. Your words do have a direct effect on the outcomes of others around you, an organization, and yourself.

The Power of Positive Words provides insights of how words create and shape values, outcomes, timing, endurance, attitude, impact, and powerful truths. May this book serve as a reminder that our words are more than just what we speak. Rather, our words play a significant role in our outcomes toward success or failure.

Stan Toler

Part 1

THE TRUTH
ABOUT WORDS

Chapter One

WORDS CREATE

Words have the power to shape reality, so we must learn to
evaluate the intention behind the words we say and hear.

----

*"Words are singularly the most powerful force
available to humanity. We can choose to use this
force constructively with words of encouragement,
or destructively using words of despair. Words have
energy and power with the ability to help, to heal, to
hinder, to hurt, to harm, to humiliate and to humble."*

YEHUDA BERG[1]

Sir Paul McCartney, bass guitarist and singer for the Beatles, was
going through a difficult time in the late 1960s. The Beatles were
on the verge of breaking up. He was agitated, "living hard and playing hard," as he put it.

One night he went to bed, exhausted, and somewhere between
deep sleep and insomnia, he had a comforting dream about his mother,
who had died when he was only fourteen. Although he had not seen
her for fourteen years, he saw his mother clearly, especially her eyes. She
said to him very gently, reassuringly, "Let it be."

Later when he awoke, he had a great feeling, like she had visited
him at this difficult point in his life and had given him this message:
"Be gentle, don't fight things, just try and go with the flow and it will
all work out."

Being a musician, he went right to the piano and started writing a song, which he titled "Let It Be." Later he played the song for the guys in the band and around a lot of people. Eventually it became the title song of an album.[2] That dream initiated a wonderful moment of creativity for him. They were certainly the right words at the right time.

You may not have had a dream that sparked great creativity. Or perhaps you have. Maybe you have a different experience of how certain words initiated creativity for you. Paul McCartney's mother's words came to him at just the right time to stir his creative energy.

POWER TO CREATE

Words do have the power to create. That is because words are not mere collections of sounds or letters. They are ideas released into the world. As such, they have creative power.

From the beginning

In the very beginning, God created the world by speaking it into existence. The ancient script tells us, "And God said, 'Let there be light,' and there was light."[3] Your words may not have the dramatic power to create the universe, but when you speak ideas they do take on power in the lives of others.

Words also have the power to destroy. In this chapter, you will understand why words have the power to shape your reality. You will also learn to evaluate the intention behind the words you say and hear.

We have all had the experience of conversing with someone and saying the wrong thing. Instead of creating a connection, we inadvertently caused the other person to put up a wall. So how can we use words to build a bridge to others?

Creating a connection

Freelance writer Jennifer Merin asked several so-called experts for tips on how they bond with people in conversation. She observed these "experts" had "the ability to express extraordinary personal charm in brilliant conversation."[4]

Modeling agency guru and image-builder extraordinaire Eileen Ford confessed she doesn't do all the talking. "Mostly, I ask questions," she said. "Really, the most important thing is to express a keen and genuine interest in the people you're speaking with."

Malachy McCourt, Irish actor, writer, and politician, likes to seed his conversations with witty expressions that show interest in the other person. He declared, "They say there are ten words that always make people laugh. Of the two I can recall, one is 'Irish.' And the other is 'prunes.' And remember there's a big difference between blarney and baloney. Blarney comes from the heart, but baloney is from the mouth."

The late Rev. Jerry Falwell said his communication skills came from his genuine love of people and his desire to help them. "In the pulpit, I preach to the lost person, the underdog, the one who is in deep personal trouble and doesn't know why another day is worth living. My goal is to let them know they are important to me and to God. To make a person aware that he or she is of great importance to you, you must show genuine interest."

He went on to say, "They won't share if you don't care. As quickly as possible, make people know that you care about their accomplishments and their burdens...and it's got to be genuine."

What Merin endeavored to show in these examples is that learning to be a good conversationalist "wins friends, influences people and brings success in professional and personal life."[5]

What did all these conversational experts try to create with their words? Not only with words but also by body language and good listening skills they created a bridge of communication, understanding, and caring. When we show sincere interest in others, we open the gate to cross such a bridge.

Words shape your reality

Henry Ford said, "The man who thinks he can and the man who thinks he can't are both right. Which one are you?"[6]

His statement is true because the way we think determines the way we act. The words that flow through our minds determine what is real. Before you ever speak a word, you think that word in your mind. Sometimes people complain that a friend or coworker "speaks before he thinks." It may seem to be true, but in some miraculous way, even faster than we realize, the words originate in our minds before our lips utter them.

Scientists believe the human mind is capable of far more than we may think. Studies done on a mouse brain reveal that it contains seventy million neurons, while a human brain contains a thousand times that many neurons. Neuroscientists have created three-dimensional images of a mouse brain that compare to the size of a grain of salt. The data within that tiny segment is about one hundred terabytes, the equivalent of twenty-five thousand high-definition movies.[7]

If this boggles your minds, as it does mine, just think of the vast potential in the human brain for thinking positive thoughts or for contemplating negative ideas. Whichever one we major on determines the reality we believe about ourselves.

Perhaps you have heard the parable of the two wolves. It is based on the idea that within every person are two wolves, who are constantly fighting each other. The good wolf represents things like kindness, courage, love, truthfulness. The bad wolf represents things like hatred, fear, lying, cheating, cruelty. There's no big secret to which one dominates your life. It's the one you feed.[8]

The words we speak to ourselves in our thoughts arise from these positive and negative forces within us. They have been fed by what we read, what we watch on television, and how past relationships have affected us. Those whose parents have affirmed them and encouraged them are more likely to grow up with positive self-talk. They face life with greater confidence. Those who grew up with parents who criticized, condemned, and insulted them, instilling feelings of failure, are more inclined to suffer from negative self-talk.

We can learn to reject the negative self-talk. People can learn to have a positive self-image, but it takes more work if our early input has been negative.

Paul J. Meyer said, "Whatever you vividly imagine, ardently desire, sincerely believe, and enthusiastically act upon must inevitably come to pass."[9] That's more than a catchy affirmation. You will notice it begins with imagining, thinking, forming words in our minds that inspire us and eventually lead to action.

Words shape other people's reality

Just as your internal speech affects your reality, you have the power to shape other people's reality by the way you talk to them. Parents have the first opportunity to affirm us by the words they use.

Lee Strobel, who was an award-winning legal editor for the *Chicago Tribune*, hungered to hear his father say, "Lee, I'm proud of you. You're really special to me. Son, I really like who you are."

Strobel admits his father may have tried to communicate such feelings in other ways, but it would have meant so much to *hear* it. Lee is sure his own workaholism through the years was an effort to heal the wound created by the lack of affirmation and an effort to earn his father's respect.

His father died while Lee was in law school. He flew back home for the wake and was amazed at the people who stopped by to greet him and say such things as: "Are you Wally's son? Oh, he was so proud of you...When you went off to Yale Law School, he was just thrilled. When you'd have a byline in the *Tribune*, he was always showing it to everybody. He couldn't stop talking about you! You were such an important part of his life."[10]

However, his father had not told him these things. He did not know until his father was dead. We can only guess at how it might have changed his life had he known these things when his father was alive.

It is all too easy to ignore people we should recognize, bypass people we should notice, or fail to affirm people who need our encouragement.

It's amazing how the right words can create a new reality in the workplace. Paul White, a psychologist who has specialized in working with businesses, families, and organizations for many years, asserts that by effectively communicating appreciation to your staff, you can create a more positive work environment: "You help not only the team members, but even the supervisors and leaders enjoy work more because they have fewer disgruntled team members and employees."[11] He says it contributes to longevity in the organization and provides better customer service because staff is more engaged.

Words can create relationships

Before you can create relationships you must be open to them. Judson Swihart described people who are not open to relationships:

> Some people are like medieval castles. Their high walls keep them safe from being hurt. They protect themselves emotionally by permitting no exchange of feelings with others. No one can enter. They are secure from attack. However, inspection of the occupant finds him or her lonely, rattling around the castle alone. The castle-dweller is a self-made prisoner. He or she needs to feel loved by someone, but the walls are so high that it is difficult to reach out or for anyone else to reach in.[12]

If that describes you, then my best advice is to get out of your castle. Lower the drawbridge, cross the moat, and dare to interact with others.

Les Parrott III and his wife Leslie started offering a course at Seattle Pacific University several years ago that promised to answer questions openly and honestly about family, friends, dating, and sex. In other words, its purpose was to teach the basics of good relationships.

At the time, Les said, it was difficult to find a course in any college or university anywhere on how to have good relationships. He was a psychologist and Leslie a marriage and family therapist. They had stacks of relationship research that showed, with a little help "most of us can make our poor relationships better and good relationships great."[13]

While a college course on the subject would be ideal, all of us can learn to develop good relationships if we're determined to do so.

Saying the right thing at the right time is an invaluable skill to cultivate. If you say the wrong thing at the wrong time, you alienate the very people you love or at least want to get to know better.

How much you value a relationship will dictate how hard you work at making it better. Leonard Sweet tells about flying to a speaking engagement in Phoenix, where his friend Tom Wiles picked him up at the airport in his red Ford Ranger pickup. They began to talk about trucks and laughed at the bumper-sticker truism: "Nothing is more beautiful than a man and his truck."

Later as he climbed into Tom's truck for the ride back to the airport, Sweet noticed two big scrapes by the passenger door. "What happened here?" he asked.

"My neighbor's basketball post fell on the truck and left those dents and white scars," Tom mourned.

"How awful! This truck is so new I can smell it."

"What's even worse is my neighbor doesn't feel responsible for the damage."

Sweet was indignant. "Did you get your insurance company to contact his insurance company? How are you going to get him to pay for it?"

Tom confessed that after a lot of soul-searching and discussions with his wife about hiring an attorney, it finally came down to this: he could either be in the right, or he could be in a relationship with his neighbor. "Since my neighbor will probably be with me longer than this truck, I decided that I'd rather be in a relationship than be right. Besides, trucks are meant to be banged up, so I got mine initiated into the real world a bit earlier than I expected."[14]

Wow! Now that is a person who values relationships. Tom could have ranted and raved, cursed, nursed a grudge, given his neighbor the cold shoulder or a hot tongue-lashing. Instead he put the relationship ahead of his feelings about the damage to his truck.

It goes along with what I read somewhere: "Keep skid chains on your tongue: always say less than you think. How you say it often counts more than what you say."[15]

People may forget what you say, but they'll never forget how you say it. And they will never forget how it made them feel.

THE RIGHT WORDS AT THE RIGHT TIME

The ancient wise man said, "There is a time for everything, and a season for every activity under the heavens: a time to be born and a time to die...a time to be silent and a time to speak."[16]

Have you heard of Job? He was a wealthy man who lived in the Middle East in the second millennium BC and had a big family—ten children in all. He owned seven thousand sheep, three thousand camels, five hundred donkeys, and five hundred yoke of oxen. You can imagine how many servants it took to care for all his livestock and tend his fields.

But Job fell on hard times. One day, marauding tribes swooped down and stole all his oxen and donkeys and killed the servants tending these animals. One servant escaped to give Job the bad news.

Then another servant arrived, giving Job the message that lightning had struck his fields, burning up the sheep and the servants who cared for them. A third messenger came, informing Job that three raiding parties had swept down on his camels, making off with them and killing his servants.

Can you believe it? Another messenger arrived with the tragic news that a tornado had caused the house to collapse where his sons and daughters had gathered for a feast. All his children were dead.

As if that weren't enough, Job became afflicted with painful sores from head to foot. Meanwhile, his wife, doubtless suffering her own grief from the loss of her children, told him he would be better off dead.

Then three friends showed up to comfort Job. It's commendable that they dropped everything else to come and visit their friend. When other family members and friends had abandoned Job, they stayed by his side, saying nothing. That was a good plan. Sometimes the best thing to say is nothing.

But after a while, the silence got to them and they began to speak, one after another, and they did what too many try to do in times of tragic sorrow: they tried to find reasons for the tragedy and assign blame for the loss.

There's a time to speak and a time to keep silent. They did well when they were silent. They were miserable comforters when they spoke.[17]

Obviously, whether trying to comfort suffering friends or trying to motivate a work force, we want to speak the right words at the right time. We want to connect with friends, neighbors, family members, or employees in a way that builds people up, not that tears them down.

Words of affirmation

Saying or writing some positive thought to a friend or coworker goes a long way toward creating a feeling of well-being in that person. Hans Finzel even created an "affirmation continuum" to illustrate how different people require different kinds of affirmation.[18] At one end of the continuum are the "desperados," which Finzel describes as people who can't get enough praise. They are desperate for words of approval. "'Warm fuzzy' is their middle name," he says. Some people especially need it when they are new to the job and are looking for evidence they are accepted and that they're doing a good job.

At the other end of the continuum are the "auto-pilots." He calls these people "Energizer Bunnies." If you try to praise them or give them a compliment, they brush it off as if it's a pesky gnat buzzing around their head. Or such a person may be skeptical and wonder why you're buttering them up. Or they wonder what you really want.

In between are the "up-and-downers," those who seem to go through peaks and valleys. Sometimes they're fine. They work well and don't need a thing. But when they hit a snag, they really need to be propped up with words of encouragement. You know who these people are in your life, whether they're family members or coworkers, and your words of affirmation make all the difference in the world to them. You create a new reality for them every time you affirm them.

Finzel suggests there are actually "normal" people, the many folks who putter through life without an apparent need to be affirmed. However, the more you think about it, the more you realize that, as John Ortberg says, "Everybody's normal until you get to know them."[19]

According to Tom Peters, the management excellence guru, "We wildly underestimate the power of the tiniest personal touch. And of all personal touches, I find the short, handwritten 'nice job' note to have the greatest impact."[20] He cited a former boss who took about fifteen minutes a day to jot a half-dozen notes to people with whom he had interacted through the day. He was astonished by the people who would later thank him for thanking them.

Words of affirmation create an atmosphere of encouragement.

Words of confidence

The renowned Italian tenor Enrico Caruso was a person of great confidence. But at the beginning of his career, he was uncertain. One opening night at the opera, Caruso was standing in the wings, waiting to go onstage, when he had an attack of stage fright. He felt his throat was constricted. He began to perspire and actually shake with fear.

The stagehands nearby heard him say, in little more than a whisper, "Out! You miserable 'little me,' get out of my way! Out! Out!"

"By that tremendous effort of will," Norman Vincent Peale observed, "Caruso was changing his self-image."[21] He changed his fear into confidence, went onstage, and sang as only Caruso could.

That's a wonderful illustration of using words to change your own reality. But how can we instill confidence in others? How do we give them the boost they need to overcome their fears and insecurities?

Of course, parents are the best equipped to do this if they will instill what Bobb Biehl calls "life confidence" or "core confidence" when children are young. This happens when parents give a child unconditional love and affirmation for what she or he has done. This does not mean the parents never discipline their children. All good parents set boundaries and establish consequences when a child crosses those boundaries.

At the same time, when a child does something positive, Biehl says, parents should affirm their children with words like, "That was good; you really did a great job on that; that's pretty; that's nice; that's wonderful."[22]

When children grow up in this kind of environment—rather than an atmosphere of yelling, criticism, and negative comments—they develop confidence. Unfortunately, many children do grow up in negative environments and come to adulthood putting on a "mask of confidence."

When we live or work with those who do not have true confidence, it becomes all the more important to give words of praise, of gratitude, or affirmation when a family member or coworker does something well. If you are the boss, it can be crucial.

Charles Pitts, the man whose company built the Toronto subway, said, "When you ride up to a site and find fifty or a hundred people standing there waiting for the boss to make a decision, you don't call a committee meeting. You get them busy immediately. If you don't know exactly what to do, you at least get them doing something that won't hurt. People have got to feel the boss knows what ought to be done."

Fred Smith, commenting on Pitts's observations, said, "A leader simply must have the confidence to lead. You can't afford to get confused in front of your people. If you want to be confused, do it at home! Confusion, like prayer, is best in a closet."[23]

Confidence builds confidence. If you're confident—as long as you're not cocky and overconfident—you will instill confidence in those around you. Your actions as well as your words can boost the confidence of your coworkers, friends, and family members. Let them know you believe in them, that you trust them, that you know they can do it.

Words of confidence create feelings of security.

Words of humility

Is it possible to *create* humility with words? I believe it's possible to *express* humility. For instance, Winston Churchill led the nation of Great Britain through World War II, from which they emerged victorious. People often gave him credit for inspiring the nation to persevere. During his eightieth birthday address to Parliament on November 30, 1954, Churchill reflected on his role in leadership: "I have never accepted what many people have kindly said—namely that I inspired the nation. Their will was resolute and remorseless, and as it proved, unconquerable. It fell to me to express it. It was the nation and the race dwelling all round the globe that had the lion's heart. I had the luck to be called upon to give the roar."[24]

That incident certainly gave Churchill the chance to *express* a humble attitude. But what words could we use to *create* humility? David McKenna, who served as president of two colleges and a seminary during his career, remembers his seven-year-old son's question shortly after his first inauguration as a college president. It was in the early 1960s and the lad asked, "Daddy, is President Kennedy great?"

"Yes," McKenna answered, "he is a great president."

The boy hesitated a moment and asked, "Well, you're a president. Why aren't you great?"[25]

We have all had the experience of being made to feel humble when a family member confronts us with the reality of who we are. But that isn't quite the same as *creating* humility. We do have to be careful about assuming a humble persona. That can too easily degenerate into pride over our humility.

As Lisa Edmondson pointed out, "A talented trumpeter who toots his own horn winds up playing to an empty theatre. A talented trumpeter who lets others recognize his talent winds up a legend."[26]

Perhaps we come close to creating humility when the word picture we create produces feelings of humility in the person who hears us. For instance, William Beebe, the naturalist, used to tell a story about Teddy Roosevelt. The two men would go out on the lawn at Sagamore Hill in the evening and search the skies for a certain spot of light near the great square of Pegasus. Then Roosevelt would recite: "That is the spiral galaxy in Andromeda. It is as large as our Milky Way. It consists of a hundred billion suns. It is one of a hundred billion galaxies." Then, with a grin, he would say, "Now I think we are small enough! Let's go to bed."[27]

That sets an example *and* speaks words intended to create and inspire humility.

Words of peace

On the island of Oahu, Hawaii, visitors saw a slogan decorating hotels and restaurants in early December 1941: "A World of Happiness in an Ocean of Peace." Amid the fragrant flowers and warm surf of the Pacific, who could imagine anything but peace? The word *pacific* even means "having a soothing effect; peaceable." Many residents of Honolulu didn't even lock their doors. It was a world of happiness in an ocean of peace.

Then on December 7, 1941, the Japanese attacked Pearl Harbor and peace disappeared.[28]

The night before he died in Warm Springs, Georgia, Franklin D. Roosevelt wrote, "We seek peace—enduring peace. We must cultivate the science of human relations—the ability of all peoples, of all kinds, to live together and work together, in the same world at peace."

President Dwight D. Eisenhower titled the second volume of his memoirs *Waging Peace*. And President John F. Kennedy said in his inaugural speech in 1961, "Let us never negotiate out of fear, but let us never fear to negotiate." And the motivation? Peace is more rewarding than war.[29]

Nobody questions we need peace in our world, peace in our families, and peace in the marketplace. Amiel Handelsman suggests some simple ways to improve relationships and create peace among your coworkers.[30]

- Apologize. Especially if you have done something in the past that hurt or offended your coworker. A sincere word of apology can make a big difference.

- Say thanks. Be on the lookout for even little things the other person does that are meaningful to you. Be specific as to what you appreciate.

- Have a conversation for relationship. In other words, "speak genuinely and listen openly." Just spending time with an individual means a great deal.

- Turn toward them. Whenever it is feasible to do so, turn to them for help. Ask a question. Be open to their suggestions.

- Stop doing something that bothers them. If you know this person has a pet peeve, don't do it.

- Acknowledge changes they have made. When they do something positive, acknowledge it. You don't need to compare it with former behavior. But recognize the positive result.

How much better will life be at home and at work when your words contribute toward an atmosphere of peace? Words of peace create an atmosphere of calmness.

Words of wisdom

English poet Samuel Taylor Coleridge wrote, "Common sense in an uncommon degree is what the world calls wisdom."[31] Yet, as we all know, common sense is very uncommon.

Several years ago, authorities confiscated quite a menagerie of reptiles in an undercover sting in Kentucky that was part of a crackdown on the venomous snake trade. Included in the raid were forty-two copperheads, eleven timber rattlesnakes, three cottonmouth water moccasins, a western diamondback rattlesnake, two cobras, and a puff adder. Altogether—a deadly bunch of critters.

As a part of the sting, undercover officers bought more than two hundred illegal reptiles. Some were advertised on websites. Jim Harrison, director of the Kentucky Reptile Zoo, said, "You can purchase anything off the Internet except common sense."[32]

Like common sense, wisdom is very uncommon. Wisdom is more than knowledge. Knowledge is the accumulation of facts we have stored in our brains. Wisdom is knowing what to do with the knowledge, especially how to apply it to life. Most of the people I consider to be wise have had some life experience. Life has taught them that some things work and some other things don't work. Theodore Roosevelt said, "Wisdom is nine-tenths a matter of being wise in time. Most of us are too often wise after the event."[33]

That's true, of course. But perhaps it's true because we learn from the event. Fortunate are we if we think of the wise thing to do or say during the event, on the spur of the moment, in real time. However, we don't need to hang our heads if our wisest ideas come after reflecting on what happened, what was said, and what was done.

Life lessons teach us common sense. When words of wisdom are spoken, people often think, *Of course, why didn't I think of that?* It seems so obvious after we hear someone say it. Yet those commonsense people are the ones to whom others turn with their questions because the answers are so wise.

Words of wisdom create a sense of assurance and well-being.

Words of encouragement

Everybody can be an encourager. All you have to do is look beyond yourself and say something positive about another person.

Truett Cathy, founder of Chick-fil-A restaurants, was a great believer in encouragement. He said, "Do you know how you can tell when a person needs encouragement? If he is breathing! We all need encouragement. I get a lot of encouragement, but I never got an overdose."[34]

Charles Schwab would have agreed with that statement. He believed that no one "could do real work except under the stimulus of encouragement and enthusiasm, and the approval of the people for whom he is working."[35]

Young Tommy had a difficult time in school. He couldn't seem to keep up with the other students and failed every time he tried something. His teacher gave up on him. She told his mother he would never amount to much because he just couldn't learn.

However, Tommy's mother was a nurturer. Furthermore, she did not give up easily. So she began teaching him at home. Every time he failed, she encouraged him. She gave him hope.

Tommy grew up to be an inventor. Eventually he held more than a thousand patents. You may know him as the one who invented the phonograph and the first commercially practical incandescent electric lightbulb. Yes, you guessed it: young Tommy was Thomas Edison, who, like most of us, thrived on encouragement.[36]

Words of encouragement create an atmosphere in which people can thrive.

No question about it: words create. What words will you use to create a better life for yourself and others?

Chapter Two

WORDS HAVE VALUE

Words represent a reality—an idea, a vision,
a concept. Learn to value the words you say and hear.

"Value your words. Each one may be the last."
STANISLAW LEC, POLISH POET[1]

There's an old story about some Oxford students who heard that
Rudyard Kipling, author of *The Jungle Book* and *Kim*, earned ten
shillings per word as an author. So they sent him ten shillings and
asked for one of his very best words. Kipling cleverly responded with
one word: THANKS.

Some years ago a writer in Santa Barbara, California, wondered
how best-selling authors today would respond to a similar query, so he
sent a letter to selected celebrity writers and included a crisp, new one-
dollar bill, saying: "I understand you get one dollar for each word you
write. Please find enclosed a dollar for one word."

Fifteen of thirty writers responded. Robert Ludlum, spy-thriller
author who wrote the Jason Bourne stories, returned the dollar and
sent a handwritten note that said: "I was going to write: 'Thanks.' And
keep the buck. However, upon close examination I've come to the conclusion that it (the dollar) is entirely too clean, bright and pressed to be
authentic and therefore have concluded that you wish to put me in jail
for passing counterfeit money. Nice try, pal."

Charles Schulz, cartoonist for the *Peanuts* gang, simply wrote: RATS!

Columnist Ann Landers advised she was not as well paid as everyone thought, but "I thank you for your interest and wish you well."

Several authors mirrored Kipling and said: THANKS.[2]

When Albert Einstein was on a lecture tour in Japan in 1922, he stayed at the Imperial Hotel in Tokyo. A bellhop delivered a message to his room and waited while the genius went through his pockets, trying to find coins for a tip. He came up empty and gave the bellhop a couple of notes as a gratuity. One note said, "A calm and modest life brings more happiness than the pursuit of success combined with constant restlessness." The other said simply, "Where there's a will, there's a way."

A relative of the bellhop brought the notes, written in German, to an auction house in Jerusalem. The prediction was they would bring less than $10,000. The final sale price was $1.8 million. His words were valuable.[3]

How much are your words worth? Probably not a million dollars. Ten shillings, like Kipling? That's about seventy cents in today's money. Your words may never get auctioned off and you may not get paid by the word, but I assure you, your words have value.

WHAT MAKES WORDS VALUABLE?

To say something has value may mean it has a monetary worth of some amount. It may mean you could exchange goods, services, or money for it. It may also mean it is intrinsically valuable or desirable. For instance, your family relationships have a value that is too great to be measured in money.

Who can put a price on the first words of a child? To hear your own son or daughter say "Mama" or "Dada" for the first time can send you rushing to phone grandparents or siblings with the exciting news, "She can talk! She said her first words!"

What about the words of a sweetheart, the first time they say, "I love you"? Simple words, but they make the heart flutter and provide a flood of warmth that you may remember the rest of your life.

Words not only have value; they can add value. You can make a person feel ten feet tall by speaking the right words at the right time. Unfortunately, words can diminish value as well. Words of criticism can bite, cut, and deflate.

We have all heard the statement, "A picture is worth a thousand words." It's true that some things are better experienced in person rather than reading a thousand words trying to describe them. More than a hundred years ago, the Piqua (Ohio) Auto Supply House ran an advertisement that said, "One Look is Worth a Thousand Words." They claimed that one look at their Firestone, Republic, Miller, or United States tires could tell the customer more than a hundred personal letters or advertisements. They claimed there was no point in buying from a catalog when one look at their tires would be convincing.[4]

So, words alone can't do everything, but they are amazingly powerful.

Consider the motivation

The value of words is affected by the motivation that sends the words our way. What is the intent behind the words?

Words meant to help. I heard as a child the old adage, "Sticks and stones may break my bones, but words can never hurt me." I'm sure adults told us that to help us learn to shake off taunts, jeers, and insults. Children are infamous for name-calling and teasing others with their words.

The truth is that the wrong words, meant to pierce and deflate, can damage far more permanently than sticks and stones. All the more reason to learn how to deal with them when critics send missiles and bombs in our direction.

Katie Couric advises young people not to take critics and their negativity to heart. "There are many people who will try to stand in your way, even cut you off at the knees, but it is often more about them than about you. Learning this early on helped me believe in myself, even when some around me did not."[5]

Everyone faces criticism now and then. So it's all the more meaningful when we know someone's words are meant to help. June Masters Bacher once wrote about receiving a greeting the day before Valentine's

Day. The card was designed with forget-me-nots and was addressed to "A Special Friend." The unsigned card said, "Just another chance to tell you in secret what you have meant in my life."[6] What gracious words, obviously meant to help.

Words meant to reassure. Words that are meant to reassure are extremely valuable. Martha Dunagin Saunders suggested several reassuring scenarios that owe their value to three little words: "I'll be there."[7] Consider the promise in response to these announcements:

"Grandma, I'm graduating in June!" *I'll be there.*

"Honey, I'm stuck at the office and can't get to the airport to meet my sister!" *I'll be there.*

"Mom, the baby cries all night, and if I don't get some sleep I'll perish!" *I'll be there.*

Saunders recalled that Elizabeth, the queen mother of England, really knew how to "be there" in World War II. During the blitz in London in 1940, when many parents were sending their children out of London to safer locations in the countryside, someone asked her if the young princesses, Elizabeth and Margaret Rose, would leave the country for their own safety. The queen replied: "The children will not leave unless I do. I shall not leave unless their father does, and the king will not leave the country in any circumstances whatever."[8]

Who could place a value on those words that communicated such reassurance to the British people?

Words meant to inform. Most of the words we use are meant to inform, and for that reason they are valuable. You can use words to reveal the truth or to conceal it. There may be occasions when concealing certain unpleasant facts is warranted. But usually we want to inform because we have something to say, a message to convey, some truth to enlighten others.

Sydney J. Harris observed that while we often use *information* and *communication* interchangeably, "they signify quite different things. Information is *giving out*; communication is *getting through*."[9]

For people living in the information age, we are nearly overwhelmed with facts. We have more information at our fingertips than ever before in history. The Internet is flooded with all kinds of data.

What used to fill up libraries is now available on microchips. What used to take hours to track down in musty encyclopedias is now available in seconds on your phone. Yet with all that information, you are especially attentive when you spot your grandchildren on Facebook. Although they live in another state, there they are in the palm of your hand, kicking another soccer goal or performing in the school choir. Words—and pictures—that inform.

All the more reason, when we have something to say, it should include words that inform. Plato said, "Wise men talk because they have something to say; fools because they have to say something."[10] Let's be wise.

Consider how they make you feel

Some of the greatest speeches in the world are those that brought forth emotion from the listeners. That seldom happens by chance. It's almost always intentional. Winston Churchill said, "Before the orator can inspire audiences with emotion, he must be swayed by it himself." He continued, "When he would rouse their indignation his heart is filled with anger. Before he can move their tears his own must flow. To convince them he must himself believe."[11]

Those who don't speak to hundreds or thousands nevertheless speak to ones and twos, such as parents who have occasionally blundered and made their children feel less than stellar. Jo Anne Lyon didn't bother to get down on her son Mark's eye level when he eagerly handed her his first kindergarten report card. She quickly pulled it from the envelope and read it while standing.

Although the report card held more than twenty items, her eyes fell on the two or three areas for improvement. Immediately she looked down on Mark and described what he needed to do to improve. His eyes clouded with disappointment as he looked up and said, "Can't I do anything right?"

Pain stabbed her heart and she quickly fell to the couch and pulled him into her arms. They went through the report card item by item together. "After the affirmations," she admitted, "the areas for improvement were reachable."[12]

Had she not quickly realized her mistake and rushed to correct the situation, imagine how Mark would have felt all evening—and perhaps for the rest of his life.

Carl Buechner said, "They may forget what you said, but they will never forget how you made them feel."[13]

Your words hold immense value in direct proportion to how you make a person feel.

NONVERBAL COMMUNICATION

As important as words are, nonverbal communication is also extremely significant. Think about what Jo Anne Lyon conveyed from her adult height, looking down on her kindergarten son. Dropping to the couch and pulling him close to her spoke volumes.

Nonverbal communication is a science all its own. People who study our nonverbals tell us we communicate many things without saying a word. Or what we do while we're speaking or while the other person is speaking also communicates a great deal.

For instance, eye contact, how frequently we look at the other person, our blink rate, frequency of glances, pupil dilation. All these things are significant. Our voice quality is also important. The rate at which we speak, the pitch, the volume, the speaking style all say something to the person who knows how to interpret such things.

Other factors include your body position, how you sit, how you stand, whether you cross your arms—these, too, are meaningful.

Perhaps you're thinking: How am I supposed to remember all these things? How can I possibly relax and be myself if I have to remember all this? Fortunately, we're interested primarily in words. So, while nonverbals are important, we're focusing on the words you use.

As business philosopher Jim Rohn said, concerning a common nonverbal way of communicating, "It's okay to send flowers, but don't let the flowers do all the talking. Flowers have a limited vocabulary. About the best flowers can say is that you remembered. But your words tell the rest."[14]

WHAT CHEAPENS WORDS?

If we agree that words are valuable, would you also agree that our messages can be cheapened by the words we use and how we use them? Let's think about a few ways we cheapen words.

Words of insincerity

Remember that Dr. Seuss book, *Horton Hatches the Egg*? It tells the improbable story of Horton the elephant, who took the responsibility of sitting on the egg laid by Mayzie, an irresponsible bird. At one point, the narrator tells us, "Horton was lonely, he wanted to play but he sat on the egg and continued to say, 'I meant what I said and I said what I meant...An elephant's faithful one hundred percent.'"[15]

Besides teaching responsibility, the story illustrates Horton's honesty and sincerity.

If you look up a definition of *sincere,* you will probably find something like "genuine, true." A jeweler can tell the difference between a diamond and a piece of glass. The average person might be fooled by their appearance, but the jeweler knows what to look for to tell the difference. A jeweler knows a diamond has a sparkle that distinguishes it from glass. It also has strength and endurance. And a price tag!

People can sometimes look very good and speak even better. Words roll off their tongue smoothly. But if you ever discover their words are not true, not spoken in absolute honesty, you will be disappointed. What happens to the value of their words? The value takes a nose dive.

Fred Smith, speaking about salespersons, said a friend told him, "The most important thing in selling is to be sincere. The other person must believe *you* believe what you're saying, even though *he* may not believe what you're saying."[16]

We highly value the words of a sincere person.

Words of carelessness

People find untold ways to be careless. Careless about their driving. Careless about their finances. Careless about their relationships. And careless about their words.

If people are careless about their driving, they can sign up for a remedial course. If they're careless about their finances, courses are available to teach them to be more responsible in handling money.

If they're careless about relationships, they can turn that around and begin to show kindness and consideration to others.

But if we're careless about our words, people soon wonder if they can trust us. Can they believe what we say? Are we truly honest persons? The value of our words begins to tank because of carelessness.

George Washington Carver, the prominent botanist who devised a hundred products using the peanut—including dyes, plastics, and gasoline—said, "How far you go in life depends on you being tender with the young, compassionate with the aged, sympathetic with the striving and tolerant of the weak and the strong. Because someday in life you will have been all of these."[17]

So we need to watch how we talk to the young, the aged, those who are striving, the weak, and the strong. If our words are careful and kind, they will be worth so much more.

Words of negativity

We're attracted to people whose words are positive because they lift us, inspire us, and transform us into more positive people. Negative words do the opposite. Michael J. Fox, speaking on coping with adversity, said, "Anything you lose will be replaced by something. You just have to be open to it. It was only when I could accept the fact that I had Parkinson's disease that I began to think, 'What haven't I lost?' I haven't lost my enthusiasm. I haven't lost my intelligence. I haven't lost my passion for life, my love of my family, my curiosity."[18]

Imagine how differently we would feel if Fox's words were full of negativity. Suppose he had said, "I don't understand why I have this disease. Why me? I've lost everything. I have no purpose in living. I have no passion for anything."

I guarantee you, his popularity would plunge because nobody wants to hear negative talk. We may sympathize with those who are going through tough times. But then we try to change the subject, or be more cheerful, or help them see that they still have much for which to be grateful.

Knowing this is how you feel when negative talk depresses you, help your words (and your reputation) keep their value by being positive, speaking positively, and being a person who brightens every room she enters.

Words of profanity

If you bring up the subject of public profanity in some circles, you may be branded as prudish. After all, everybody's using bad language these days, right?

We have watched as the walls of good taste have gradually fallen. First words that polite company would never use started creeping into movies. Then they crept into television, first on premium channels, then cable, and then broadcast TV. "It's like an itch that can't be scratched enough," Brent Bozell says, "forever pushed to the next level."[19]

Cartoonist Charles Schultz of *Peanuts* fame said, "I have a strong dislike for vulgar phrases and find that the terms 'good grief' and 'rats' will cover virtually anything that happens."[20]

By monitoring our words, we can avoid cheapening them.

Sheer volume of words

A friend's son collected bicentennial quarters. Older readers may remember when the 1976 edition of the American quarter was popularly produced during the United States' bicentennial year. Some ten or twelve years later, when the son went to college, he needed money to buy a camera for a class on photography. Ready cash was not available, so he contacted a coin collector and asked how much bicentennial quarters were worth. The expert said, "Twenty-five cents." He went on to predict that's all they would ever be worth because so many of them were minted.

A profusion of words also tends to make them less valuable.

Words often mean less due to the sheer quantity that flows from some people's mouths. It's like they cannot find the shutoff valve. A man and woman, both residents in a senior citizens' high-rise, sat near each other in the lobby of their building. She was a talker. He would have been happy to sit in silence. But she, who lived alone and had someone to talk to only when she came to the lobby or attended one of the facility's social events, continued to talk. Her words spilled out in a stream of consciousness about subjects that meant nothing to her lone listener.

Finally, when she paused to take a breath, he turned to her and said, "You talk too much." It was blunt, but there it was, his succinct analysis. She was offended, but it stopped her, at least temporarily. She attributed his frank remark to his "playing with less than a full deck." But he certainly knew enough to call her out on her incessant flow of words.

Someone said, "Blessed is he who having nothing to say cannot be persuaded to say it."

Make your words count and increase their value by choosing them carefully. Less is more.

HOW TO MAKE YOUR WORDS WORTH MORE

Is it possible to increase the value of your words? I believe it is.

Choose your words carefully

Archimedes, the Greek mathematician who lived in the third century BC, declared if he had a long-enough lever, a big-enough fulcrum, and a place to stand, he could move the Earth. His statement, other scientists declared, is theoretically true. But Joseph Conrad, who was a writer, not a mathematician, said, "Give me the right word with the right accent and I can take the world."[21]

Certainly, powerful words given at the right time have swayed the world. Think of Abraham Lincoln's speech at Gettysburg. It was a short speech, but we have never forgotten it because of the careful selection of his words. Or think of Martin Luther King Jr.'s 1963 speech on the National Mall in Washington, when he declared, "I have a dream…" Powerful words, carefully chosen, words that have moved people to action. Indeed, valuable words.

Communicate clearly

Communicating clearly is not as easy as it sounds. One year a trained investigator mingled with the crowds at Grand Central Station in New York City. He asked ten people the question: "What is your destination?" Admittedly, it was noisy, the height of the vacation season, but here are their responses:

1. Protestant.

2. Mind your own business.

3. I'm a shoe salesman.

4. Home, if I can find my wife.

5. I'm learning to be a mail clerk.

6. Checkers.

7. Shut your mouth!

8. I don't know you.

9. Hoboken.

10. I believe in faith, hope, and charity.[22]

Communicating clearly is sometimes difficult, but all the more reason why those who achieve it find their words more valuable.

Gerald R. Ford, thirty-eighth president of the United States, believed in the importance of communicating clearly. He said, "If I went back to college again, I'd concentrate on…learning to write and speak before an audience. Nothing in life is more important than the ability to communicate effectively."[23]

Communicating clearly increases the value of your words.

Spend your words frugally

We talked earlier about the sheer volume of words and how talking too much can cheapen them. Consequently, spending your words frugally can make them more valuable.

Calvin Coolidge is remembered as a man of few words. Long before the days of direct deposit, a courier hand-delivered his check from the Treasury Department. Hoping to get a reaction from the president upon receiving a check for that much money, the courier tried to drag out his departure from the Oval Office.

When Coolidge asked what he was waiting for, the courier admitted he was curious to see if the president had anything to say about the check. The president looked at the check, looked at the courier, and said, "Please return."

On another occasion, his reputation as "Silent Cal" was so well-known that one woman, part of a group visiting the White House for tea, said to him, "Mr. President, I have a little wager with the other ladies in our group that I can get you to say more than two words."

Coolidge said, "You lose."[24]

When you economize on your volume of words, people pay attention when you do say something. Being frugal in speech may just increase their value.

Aim your words precisely

The word *aim* implies you have a target in mind. The word *precisely* means you want to hit the target every time. Not to the right or to the left; not above or below, but right in the target. Many people have developed the habit of being careless in their speech. For instance, when everything is "awesome," nothing is awesome.

There's an old story about a small-town newspaper editor who went on vacation and left his assistants in charge. While he was gone, a tornado ripped through the town, tearing the steeple off the Baptist church, lifting the roofs from several prominent homes, and scattering debris all over town. Upon the editor's return, he was irate because his assistants had used his treasured 60-point type for the headline about the tornado.

He shouted angrily, "What did you mean by using that 60-point type for a little old tornado?" The assistants protested, "That's the biggest story ever to happen here!"

"It's the biggest story to happen here *so far*," huffed the editor. "I've been saving that type for the second coming of Christ!"[25]

You don't want to use 60-point type on a 36-point story. On the other hand, you don't want to minimize something that is truly significant. When you catch a coworker doing something well, use appropriate words of praise to call attention to their good work. When your family treats you well, let them know in precise, positive words just how much you appreciate it.

Aim your words precisely and they will increase in value.

Speak your words sincerely

As I have often said, "People may forget what you say, but they'll never forget how you say it. Be positive. Lift others up and they will follow you."

Dale Carnegie of *How to Win Friends and Influence People* fame declared, "There are four ways, and only four ways, in which we have contact with the world. We are evaluated and classified by these four contacts: what we do, how we look, what we say, and how we say it."[26]

How you say it reflects the sincerity of your heart. Abraham Lincoln understood this and was known for his ability to speak from the heart. In 1842, he spoke to the Washington Temperance Society. During that speech he made the following observation: "If you would win a man to your cause, first convince him you are his sincere friend... Assume to dictate to his judgment, or to command his action, or to make him as one to be shunned and despised, and he will retreat within himself... You shall no more be able to pierce him than to penetrate the hard shell of a tortoise with a rye straw."[27]

SHOW OTHERS YOU VALUE THEIR WORDS

If you want to show others you value their words, learn to listen. Listening is an art, but you can learn it and master it.

Matthew Sleeth, an emergency room physician, was on duty when five-year-old Maggie Plummer and her twin sister Lila came in. Maggie sat on the exam table while her father held Lila.

"Do they both have an earache?" Dr. Sleeth inquired.

"No," answered their father, "but they will. They're mirror twins and they do everything together, even getting sick. When Maggie gets an ear infection on the right, Lila will get one on the left." He paused and added, "We told them that we'll have to cancel their birthday party tomorrow." Both girls' lower lips began to tremble.

The doctor asked if he could begin by examining Lila's ears, the twin who was not complaining. They looked perfect. But when he examined Maggie, her left ear looked fine, but the right ear canal was swollen; he could not see the eardrum.

"She's got a little rock in the canal," he said. "When did this start bothering her?"

"It was after they were swimming in the pond two days ago." They first thought she had gotten water in it, but it kept getting worse, and they assumed it was an ear infection.

The doctor suctioned the ear and out came the stone. For the first time in two days, Maggie could hear out of the ear and had no pain.

Suddenly both girls looked at each other and realized the consequence of what had just happened. Their father asked, "Any reason they can't have their party tomorrow?"

Dr. Sleeth says he is not proud of how he answered the question, but he said, "No reason, as long as I get a birthday hug." He claims you haven't lived until you've been hugged by five-year-old girls who've just had their birthday party restored.[28]

Hearing is a wonderful gift that most of us take for granted. But hearing is not the same as listening. If you want to assure others that you value their words, you must do more than hear. You must listen.

Listen attentively

Diogenes was quite direct when he said, "We have two ears and one tongue so that we would listen more and talk less."[29]

Peter Drucker, the management expert, taught the importance of listening when he said, "Listening (the first competence of leadership) is not a skill, it is a discipline. All you have to do is keep your mouth shut."[30]

One of the reasons we don't listen well is that we are too eager to speak. Edgar Watson Howe joked, "No man would listen to you talk if he didn't know it was his turn next."[31] That observation, spoken in jest, is a little too close to the truth for comfort.

One such person, who was just waiting for his next opportunity to speak, called Jim Bishop one morning and began the conversation the way he always did: "Jim, how are ya?"

Jim, knowing the man seldom really listened, decided to test just how poor a listener this fellow was. So he answered, "I have lung cancer."

The man said, "Wonderful. Say, Jim…"[32] Point proved.

So why is listening such a challenge for so many of us? It has been observed that although we speak 100 to 150 words a minute, we can comprehend at 250 to 300 words a minute. But we think at 600 words a minute. So, if you are a fast listener and your friend is a slow talker, you may have 500 words a minute left over to think about other things.[33]

Margaret Wheatley said, "Listening is such a simple act. It requires us to be present, and that takes practice, but we don't have to do anything else. We don't have to advise, or coach, or sound wise. We just have to be willing to sit there and listen."[34]

Regard the speaker warmly

One way we can improve our listening skills is to pay close attention, regarding the speaker warmly. If you truly listen to the other person, it will make all the difference in the world. Paul Tillich believed, "The first duty of love is to listen."[35]

David Augsburger observed, "Being heard is so close to being loved, that for the average person, they are almost indistinguishable."[36]

How often have you been in the middle of conversation and you realized that the other person is no longer listening? They have tuned you out. How did that make you feel? Maybe you felt like little Heidi, who asked, "Momma, are you listening to me?"

Her distracted mother answered, "Um-hmm."

"No, Momma," Heidi insisted, "I need you to listen with your eyes."[37]

Listen with your eyes and you will communicate that you value the speaker's words.

Ask questions selectively

Nothing tells your friend or your spouse that you are listening carefully like asking intelligent questions. Dale Carnegie said, "Ask questions that other persons will enjoy answering. Encourage them to talk about themselves and their accomplishments. Remember that the people you are talking to are a hundred times more interested in themselves and their wants and problems than they are in you and your problem."

He illustrated, "A person's toothache means more to that person than a famine in China which kills a million people. A boil on one's neck interests one more than forty earthquakes in Africa. Think of that the next time you start a conversation."[38]

Listen carefully and ask questions selectively if you want your coworker or friend to know you value their words.

Words have value. Try to determine the speaker's true motivation if you want to have some idea of how valuable their words are. How do your words make others feel? That affects their value. Eliminate insincerity, carelessness, and negativity if you want to prevent the cheapening of your words. Be intentional, choose your words carefully, communicate them clearly, and spend them frugally if you want to increase their value. And you can signal that you value the words of others if you will learn to listen attentively and warmly.

Chapter Three

WORDS ENDURE

A word cannot be truly retracted or recalled. Once
spoken, it exists in the mind of the speaker and hearer.

---

*"A state of society where men may not
speak their minds cannot long endure."*
WINSTON CHURCHILL[1]

I f I had only known sooner." Those are often painful words, uttered
because had we known sooner, we might have made a different decision, chosen a different path, decided to do something that would have
made our lives turn out better.

Nobody knew the truth of that sentiment better than Samuel
Morse. He was an artist by trade, a painter, who had traveled to Washington, DC, in 1825 to paint the portrait of the Marquis de Lafay-
ette. While he was hard at work, painting the likeness of this great
man, the most ardent French supporter of the American Revolution,
a messenger on horseback delivered a one-line letter. It was from his
father in New Haven, Connecticut. It said simply: "Your dear wife is
convalescent."

Morse hastened to Connecticut, but by the time he arrived, his
wife had already been buried. It broke his heart to know it had taken a
week for the news to reach him about his wife's failing health and sub-
sequent death.

He immediately put aside his painting and set about developing a means of long-distance communication. He actually set up shop in the Capitol building, where he sent messages back and forth between the House and Senate wings to test his telegraph prototype. Although many senators were skeptical, he convinced them to appropriate $30,000 to build a telegraph line, spanning thirty-eight miles between Washington, DC, and Baltimore.

History chronicles that he sent his now-famous message on May 24, 1844, while a large crowd assembled inside the Capitol to witness it. Annie Ellsworth, daughter of the US patent commissioner Henry Leavitt Ellsworth, chose the message. It was a portion of Scripture from the King James Version, Numbers 23:23: "What hath God wrought?" Moments later the same four-word message was relayed back from Baltimore.[2]

That message has endured and has led to many more advanced means of communication. This is an interesting historical account for us, but it could have made all the difference in the world for Morse, had the telegraph existed before his wife's death. We'll never know, of course, but he might have been able to make it back to Connecticut before she passed.

WHAT MAKES WORDS ENDURE?

We can't remember some words long enough to repeat them after reading a single paragraph. Yet we remember other words all our lives. What makes the difference? Why are some words so significant they endure?

Words that make us remember

Here are some words I imagine you have never forgotten, because they bring back such poignant memories:

"I do."

"I now pronounce you husband and wife."

"You're hired!"

"You're fired!"

"It's a girl!" (or a boy).

"Daddy, I met this boy…"

"The diagnosis is cancer."

"I'm sorry. We did all we could."

Other words that are unique to your life experience cling to your memory and you can't forget them. Some are sheer joy. Others—you wish you could forget.

Either way, they are stored in your memory bank and are not likely to leave because they bring back vivid memories.

Words that are well-spoken or well-written

Consider these words:

"To be or not to be, that is the question"—Hamlet's famous soliloquy.

"Et tu, Brute?"—Julius Caesar's dying words.

"Beware the ides of March"—words of the soothsayer to Julius Caesar.

"Romeo, Romeo, wherefore art thou Romeo?"—Juliet's words to her lover.

We could go on, but you know, of course, what all these words have in common—they were all written by William Shakespeare, the English poet who lived from 1564 to 1616. He is arguably the best-selling fiction author of all time. His works have sold an estimated four billion copies.[3]

But why have Shakespeare's words endured? Some think it is because his plays are so adaptable. They can be interpreted in many different ways and have been adapted in various countries in various ages. Some say his plays have an openness "that allows them to be endlessly reinterpreted."[4] As Andrew Dickson says, Shakespeare's plays "were designed to be reinvented."[5]

Still others think Shakespeare has endured because of his highly believable characters. Russell Beale believes his characters are "very hospitable" to actors.[6] In addition, the British people exported Shakespeare around the world. In India, he became an important tool of indoctrination. As Dickson said, "Shakespeare was imposed on Indian children to instill British culture and values." However, the Indian people liked Shakespeare so much they rewrote his stories in their native language and often cast "the overbearing British...in highly unfavorable light."[7]

Not that Shakespeare was perfect. Beale admits the bard's imperfections but adds that "at his best he was the very best."[8]

It's one thing for Shakespeare to be outstanding through the centuries. But he's not the only one who has written and spoken memorably. What can we learn from other great speakers of the ages?

Heather Rodriguez from the Texas A&M College of Liberal Arts believes our American presidents can teach us a great deal about words that endure. She admits to analyzing "the stories and the myths that the presidents tell in trying to construct who we are as people." She continues, "What presidents say, and how they say it, gives us guidance for what our culture considers important."[9]

She says there are three ways presidents have ensured their words would live after them.

Be intentional. When Franklin D. Roosevelt guided his fellow Americans through the Great Depression, he told them the only thing they had to fear was fear itself. When John F. Kennedy wanted to challenge Americans to serve their country, he told them, "Ask not what your country can do for you. Ask what you can do for your country."

By implication both of these presidents were clear that, although it seemed they were giving their hearers a choice, there was really only one choice for an American.

Be startling. Rodriguez points out that when Richard Nixon said, "I am not a crook," and when Bill Clinton said, "I did not have sexual relations with that woman," they were being startlingly unique. No president had ever said something like that publicly.

As she observes, no other presidents had ever gotten themselves into situations where they could be asked such personal questions. So while their answers were startling, they also revealed the kind of character they believed to be important.

Be eloquent. Some presidents, when speaking on momentous occasions, rose to the occasion and said what they had to say eloquently. For instance, Abraham Lincoln, speaking in his Gettysburg address, said, "We here highly resolve that these dead shall not have died in vain." Ronald Reagan at another solemn occasion said, "The crew of the space shuttle Challenger honored us by the manner in which they lived their lives. We will never forget them, nor the last time we saw them, this morning, as they prepared for their journey and waved goodbye and 'slipped the surly bonds of earth' to 'touch the face of God.'"

These speeches are outstanding, but what other kinds of words are memorable? Moving from presidential speeches to the mundane world of catch phrases, what do we remember?

Words that are catchy

When you hear these words, what product do you think of?

"Melts in your mouth, not in your hands."

"Finger-lickin' good."

"Takes a licking and keeps on ticking."

The answers, of course, are M&Ms, Kentucky Fried Chicken, and Timex, respectively.

Try these:

"The quicker picker-upper."

"Be all you can be."

"The best part of waking up is _____ in your cup."

Again, obviously, these slogans are about Bounty, the US Army, and Folgers. These slogans are clear and concise. They "convey a clear idea in a compelling way."[10]

WORDS THAT CAN'T BE UNSPOKEN

You have likely heard of "the law of the Medes and Persians." It is an expression that means something that cannot be altered. One of the great historical examples of this deals with Daniel, a Jewish man who had been relocated from his native Israel to the land of Babylon.

As this chapter of the story opens, there's a new sheriff in town. Actually, it was a new king. The army of Darius the Mede had entered the supposedly impregnable city of Babylon, assassinated King Belshazzar, and Darius took over. The ancient script tells us he was sixty-two years old when he became the king.

In organizing the kingdom, Darius appointed 120 governors to govern all parts of his kingdom. To oversee the governors, he appointed three vice-regents. Daniel, one of the vice-regents, was so full of spirit and intelligence that he outclassed all the others. Consequently, the king appointed him in charge of the whole kingdom.

The vice-regents and governors became jealous of Daniel and tried to dig up some dirt on him to discredit him to the king. But Daniel was so exemplary in everything he did, they couldn't find any legitimate complaint against him. However, the truth has never been an obstacle to crooked politicians, so they schemed until they came up with a plan.

They approached the king and said, "We governors and vice-regents have talked about it, and we agree that you should issue a decree that for the next thirty days, no one should pray to any god or mortal except you, O king. Anybody who disobeys will be thrown into the lions' den." They continued, "Issue this decree, O king, and make it unconditional, as if written in stone like all the laws of the Medes and the Persians."[11]

Daniel was a man of faith. His detractors knew he would ignore the law, and they were watching to see if they could catch him in violation of this decree, a law of the Medes and Persians. Once spoken, once published, it could not be retracted. The law would endure.

As expected, Daniel went home and prayed in the same way he always had—with his windows open wide, praying toward his beloved Jerusalem three times a day. The conspirators overheard him praying and asking God for help.

They immediately went to the king and reminded him of the decree. The king confirmed that he had signed the decree to be effective for thirty days, and he even repeated that it was "written in stone like all the laws of the Medes and Persians."

When they told him about Daniel's violation of the decree, the king was very upset. Daniel was his main man, and the king tried all day to think of a way to get Daniel out of the predicament he was in. But the conspirators were persistent. They came back to remind the king of the irreversible law. The king had no choice but to order Daniel apprehended and thrown into the lions' den. The king had such confidence in Daniel that he told him, "Your God, to whom you are so loyal, is going to get you out of this."[12]

Long story a little shorter, Daniel survived. The lions didn't hurt him, and both the king and Daniel rejoiced because not even the law of the Medes and Persians could conquer this good man. The British pastor Charles Spurgeon reportedly said it was just as well the lions didn't try to eat Daniel because he was half grit and the other half backbone.[13]

We would be in big trouble if the law of the Medes and Persians were in effect today and we could never retract anything we said. Talk about words enduring! In truth our words do endure. But here's the good news: Although we can't fully retract our words once they're out there, we can apologize. All it takes is the courage to say six of the hardest words in the English language: "I was wrong; I am sorry." Tough to say but essential, because we're not infallible. We do sometimes say the wrong thing—intentionally or unintentionally. Fortunately, the law of the Medes and Persians is no longer in effect; we can back up, admit our words were in error, and express regret.

HOW TO MAKE YOUR WORDS ENDURE

Carmine Gallo, a Forbes online contributor, suggests if you want your words to be memorable, remember this five-word phrase: "To put it in perspective." If you are speaking in abstract terms, people will not remember what you say. But if you can come up with a way to help your listeners see your point as well as hear it, your words will be more memorable.

Reporting on the drought in California, CNN stated, "A staggering eleven trillion gallons are needed for California to recover from the emergency." Of course, eleven trillion anything is impressive, but notice how they made it memorable: "That's more than fourteen thousand times the amount of water it would take to fill the Dallas Cowboys stadium…It's the amount of water that flows over Niagara Falls in about 170 days' time."[14]

Eleven trillion is still an outrageous number, but picturing a football stadium and Niagara Falls puts it in perspective and gives us a more memorable picture of the problem.

Gallo gives another example in which a company was responsible for planting over two million trees. That's impressive, but how do you put it in perspective in such a way that people remember it? They said, "Two million trees. That's the equivalent of ninety Central Parks." If you have visited or even seen a picture of Central Park in New York, suddenly you can visualize it and remember it because they put it in perspective.

Criticism versus compliments

Is it true or does it just seem like it's easier to remember criticisms than to remember compliments? Clifford Nass, professor of communication at Stanford University says, "This is a general tendency for everyone…Some people do have a more positive outlook, but almost everyone remembers negative things more strongly and in more detail."[15]

Professor Nass says the brain handles positive and negative emotions in different hemispheres, and that negative emotions require more thinking. Consequently, we process negative thoughts more thoroughly and we tend to ruminate more about them.

Roy Baumeister, professor of social psychology at Florida State University, wrote an article titled, "Bad Is Stronger than Good," in which he said research has shown that "bad emotions, bad parents, and bad feedback have more impact than good ones. Bad impressions and bad stereotypes are quicker to form and more resistant to disconfirmation than good ones."[16]

In other words, he points out, people get more upset about losing fifty dollars than they are happy about gaining fifty dollars. All of this has bearing on which words endure and which do not. From the research these professors have done, it is obvious that negative words endure longer than positive ones.

Consequently, the old song that says, "Where never is heard a discouraging word and the skies are not cloudy all day," is apparently about a mythological place. Very few of us can point to such a place in our life experiences.

However, in the midst of discouraging words and cloudy days, a well-timed compliment may have incredibly lasting effects. Young John had to quit school at the age of twelve when his father went to prison. The lad worked in a boot-blacking factory, where he pasted labels on bottles of the blacking and tried to avoid the rats that infested the place. He dreamed of being a writer, yet how does an unknown young man with few connections break into the world of publishing?

Like many writers before and after him, John received several rejection letters. One publisher included a note with his letter, telling John he was a great writer and even said the world needed him. This encouragement sent the young man rejoicing through the streets of London. They also motivated him to continue writing.

By the way, John was his middle name. Charles John Huffam Dickens continued to write, publishing many novels, including *Oliver Twist, Great Expectations, A Tale of Two Cities,* and *A Christmas Carol.*[17] We'll never know how things might have turned out had he not received that encouraging note included with a publisher's rejection letter.

We all need encouragement. In fact, the apostle Paul said, "Encourage one another and build each other up, just as in fact you are doing" (1 Thessalonians 5:11). He even indicated some people have the gift of encouragement (Romans 12:8).

Phyllis Theroux observed, "One of the commodities in life that most people can't get enough of is compliments. The ego is never so intact that one can't find a hole in which to plug a little praise. But compliments by their very nature are highly biodegradable and tend to dissolve hours or days after we receive them—which is why we can always use another."[18]

WHICH WILL ENDURE—POSITIVE OR NEGATIVE?

Johnny Mercer was a popular singer-songwriter from the mid-1930s through the mid-1950s. He said his publicity agent had gone to hear Father Divine, a spiritual leader in the first half of the twentieth century. He told Mercer that the pastor preached a sermon in which he said, "You got to accentuate the positive and eliminate the negative."

Mercer said, "Wow! That's a colorful phrase!" And he went on to write the lyrics of a song by the name, "Accentuate the Positive." The song became very popular in 1945 and spent thirteen weeks on the *Billboard* magazine chart. It was inducted into the Library of Congress's National Recording Registry in 2015 for its "cultural, artistic and/or historical significance to American society and the nation's audio legacy."[19]

Whether you ever sing the song, you can follow its advice when it comes to your words and how they impact the relationships in your life.

Accentuate the positive

Norman Vincent Peale, who wrote *The Power of Positive Thinking* and many other books, told about a group of people who bought some land with the intention of building a great human service institution. (He never said if it was a hospital or some other kind of institution that was to have a positive life-saving or life-enhancing influence.) As plans began, some among the group were skeptical. They felt they needed more money to make it work. They said things like, "If we had more money, if we had more support, if…if…if."

Others in the group weren't convinced it could be done. They were strongly of the opinion, "It can't be done. It just can't."

Still others were even more determined. They declared, "There's no way. It is impossible, absolutely impossible."

One of the men in the group who had been quite generous in giving toward the enterprise came up with an idea. He asked for a small piece of the land they had acquired. Since he had shown his commitment to the cause, they could hardly turn him down. People were definitely surprised when he announced he wanted the small plat of land for a cemetery. Sure enough, after he had possession of the property, he fenced off the little enclosure and set up three small gravestones.

He announced a time for the burial service and the people arrived. When he unveiled the stones, this is what people saw: in one was carved the word *If*, in another *Can't*, and in the third *Impossible*. He told his friends and fellow investors, "Here lie buried words that could cause the failure of our enterprise. Leave them buried." People got the message.[20]

Without doubt, one way to accentuate the positive is to bury negative words. When negative words endure in our speech and in our thinking, we become our own worst enemies. Our thoughts and our speech patterns doom us to failure before we start because we are working against our own best interest.

Psychiatrist Smiley Blanton commented that some of his patients would think, "If only I had not done that." Or, "If only I had done that." He recommended to his patients that when they were tempted to say *if only* they should substitute the words *next time*.[21] The words we use do make a difference. Think of how much more positive it is to think about what you will do next time instead of glumly thinking, "If only I had or hadn't done that."

We have all made enough mistakes that we could fill our thoughts and our speech with complaints of "if only." If only I had taken that job when I had the chance. If only I had treated my spouse better. If only I hadn't nagged my kids so much. If only I had bought that stock when I had the opportunity. If only I hadn't sold it when I did. On and on the litany goes.

Mordecai Brown played baseball for the St. Louis Cardinals and the Chicago Cubs in the early part of the twentieth century. He was considered an elite pitcher in his era.[22] Early in his life he worked on a farm to help support his family, as a lot of other young people did in those days. One day his hand caught in some farm machinery, and he lost most of the forefinger on his right hand and badly crushed his second finger.

He could have said, "There goes my hope of being a pitcher." He might have moaned, "If only I hadn't had that accident. There go my dreams out the window. It's impossible now."

But instead he accepted it and learned to throw the ball with the fingers he had left. In time, he made a local team as a third baseman.

One day the team manager was directly behind the first baseman when Mordecai threw him the ball from third. The manager was amazed to see the twists and turns of that ball as it sped toward the first baseman's mitt.

The manager said, "Mordecai, you are a born pitcher. You have speed and control and, boy, with that gyrating ball you'll have every batter swinging but only hitting the air."[23]

And that's exactly what happened. When he pitched in the big leagues, batters were baffled when the ball danced, gyrated up and down, and slid directly over the plate. His strikeout record was impressive.

What should have been a tragedy turned into an amazing asset. The injured fingers gave him a unique advantage when he threw the ball. Instead of filling his mind and speech with *ifs* and *can'ts* and *impossibles*, he was determined to overcome the handicap. And he did.

What would happen if you too became determined to replace negative words with positive ones like *next time* and *can* and *possible*? In so doing, you will set yourself up for success by speaking words that accentuate the positive and endure constructively.

Eliminate the negative

Having said that, you may find eliminating the negative to be harder than you think. Entrepreneur John Rampton says every language contains more negative words than positive ones.[24] He contends that we seem to need many words to express our negative emotions but only a handful of words to describe our positive feelings. Researchers have discovered, he says, that most cultures have words for seven basic emotions: joy, fear, anger, sadness, disgust, shame, and guilt. That is one positive word and six negative ones. Unless we work on controlling those negative words, we will do more harm than good with our expressions. We will say many things that painfully endure to our detriment.

Stephen Shainbart, a counselor in New York City, reminds us that relationships can be damaged severely because, "Horrible words stay out there forever."[25] In other words, they endure long after you may have forgotten them. They can wound severely and heal slowly, if at all. Shainbart offers five steps to avoid worsening a relationship.

1. Don't be afraid of conflict. He contends that one of the advantages of conflict is that it brings problems out into the open. He cautions that if we always avoid conflict, it may be a sign that a relationship is less than honest and is suffering from poor communication. By avoiding conflict, we may miss the opportunity to bring encouragement to the other person, to speak words that encourage. No word can endure if it is never spoken.

2. How we fight makes all the difference. Getting angry is one thing, but spouting nasty words is another, and extremely detrimental. Even a sincere apology may fail to eliminate the pain and stain of those negative words from the mind of the injured person. Fighting with the goal of injuring the other person, shaming them, or belittling them will always result in speaking words that should be left unspoken.

3. Don't escalate an argument with overgeneralizations. When we use words like *always* and *never*, we are seldom right. Does your friend or spouse always do the thing that irritates you? Do they never get it right? We will generate less defensiveness in the other person if we zero in on specific behaviors or issues instead of overgeneralizing. Being specific may enable us to speak words that are helpful and healing. Generalizing runs the risk of exaggerating a person's faults and speaking words that injure.

4. Express interest in your partner's life. It's easy to make assumptions, to think your partner knows you care, but it's always better to show it. A simple question like, "How was your day?" can let your partner know you are sincerely interested in what they are doing, thinking, and feeling. If they have had a bad day, talking about it may provide some release of tension, especially if your attentiveness shows you care. If they have had a good day, their conversation may brighten the evening for both of you.

5. Problems get worse when you hide them. It is difficult to discuss things like financial problems, mental health difficulties, or drinking and substance abuse. But even if it causes tension, you will be better off if you get it into the open where you can discuss it. A hidden problem may embitter the person. It may become like a poison and discolor every thought. Shining the light of truth on hidden things brings them to the surface where they can be addressed.

Relationships are the places where our words can do the most good or cause the most harm. Make your words positive. Eliminate negative words and negative insinuations. Words endure. By eliminating those "horrible words" from our vocabulary and refusing to hurt others, we will go a long way toward creating relationships—as well as words—that endure.

Part 2

STRATEGIC
WORD USE

Chapter Four

FILTERING WORDS

Just as a filter is needed to remove contaminants
from drinking water, you need a filter for your words.

*"You cannot escape the result of your thoughts...
Whatever your present environment may be, you will
fall, remain, or rise with your thoughts, your vision, your
ideal. You will become as small as your controlling
desire, as great as your dominant aspiration."*

JAMES LANE ALLEN[1]

A friend tells about visiting Czechoslovakia in the early 1990s before the country divided into the two sovereign states of Czech Republic and Slovakia. In the city of Ostrava in the northeastern part of the country, he and a colleague went down to the hotel dining room early one morning and ordered coffee. The waitress served it in glass cups with no handles. It was too hot to touch, so they had to wait until it cooled enough to pick it up. As they talked, they noticed the coffee grew darker at the bottom of the cup. When they were finally able to drink it, they discovered a layer of coffee grounds in the bottom.

My friend told his colleague, "I guess coffee filters haven't made it to Ostrava yet."

A few day later in a private home near Prague, the host's wife poured coffee from a beautiful silver pot, but as my friend drank it, he discovered once again a layer of grounds in the bottom of his cup. He eventually learned they called it Turkish coffee and that's just the way they made it.

Being a creature of habit, he was glad to get back to the States and his filtered coffee.

Just as many of us prefer our coffee grounds filtered so we can enjoy our "cuppa joe" without the grit, we need a filter for our words. Is it possible to filter the words we think, hear, and speak to ensure they are true and helpful? That's what we will explore in this chapter.

THINKING THE BEST THOUGHTS

When we begin to talk about thinking, most of us are not Einsteins. By the way, when he published his papers on theoretical physics, including the theory of relativity, Einstein was a clerk in the patent office in Bern, Switzerland. Only twenty-six years old, he did not look like the white-haired older man we have come to associate with his name. He had wavy black hair and might not have impressed you if you passed him on the street. But the papers he wrote were "blazing rockets which in the dark of night suddenly cast a brief but powerful illumination over an immense unknown region," according to the physicist Louis de Broglie.[2]

Did Einstein really have a special brain that enabled him to think in a way that was superior to all others? Was the human race really divided into two groups: Albert Einstein and everybody else?

Einstein died in 1955 at the age of 76. He was cremated, all but his brain. For decades, Einstein's brain soaked in a jar of formaldehyde. In the 1980s, certain neurobiologists were able to take a few bits of gray matter from his brain and examine it. What they found was that it was just a brain—one that thought extraordinary thoughts, but physiologically it was just a brain.[3]

So there's hope for you and me. Apparently, it isn't so much the quality of the gray matter as the quality of the thoughts we conjure in the gray matter we have.

And let's face it, a lot of our thoughts are wandering, nonspecific, unfocused, and accomplish little. It's no wonder when you think of all the distractions we face from the daily bombardment of media. So we need to learn to filter our thoughts.

Filtering our thoughts

Since we don't have a literal filter, like those we use in our coffee makers or those we change in our furnaces, how do we filter our thoughts?

Get a firm grip on social media. The Division of Disability Resources and Educational Services in the College of Applied Sciences at the University of Illinois suggests ten ways we are distracted by social media.

1. Watching what everyone else is up to at the moment. If you spend a lot of time liking posts on Facebook, reading Twitter tweets, snapchatting on Snapchat, pinning on Pinterest, and surfing the Internet, you aren't getting much else done.

2. Stalking people on social media, checking to see what they're doing at any given moment.

3. Getting drawn into content that is interesting but not relevant to what you should be doing.

4. Taking Wiki-walks. In other words, you follow links in Wikipedia from one article to another. Chances are, the longer the walks, the more unrelated the articles.

5. Taking time to watch each account just to be sure you don't miss something.

6. Stopping whatever you are doing in order to respond if someone else contacts you or mentions you.

7. Having too many accounts to follow reasonably.

8. Having too many people to follow realistically.

9. Wandering the social mediasphere, aimlessly looking for relevant content.

10. Looking at what your friends have been up to all day instead of focusing on your work.[4]

How can you rein in your thoughts and stop the never-ending interruptions?

- Turn off your alerts and notifications.

- Check email only two or three times a day.

- Schedule regular blocks of time to turn off your phone.

- Create a list of the three most important priorities for today.

The hard part is turning off all social media until you accomplish those three things. Check yourself at the end of the day to see how you did, then plan for tomorrow.

If you will limit your social media time through some kind of filtering process, you will find yourself with more time to do the things you really need to do.

Limit how much you watch television. Is it true or false that reading is better for you than watching television? There's a common perception that if you curl up with a good book, you're an intellectual, but if you binge-watch Netflix, you're a couch potato. What's the truth?

Studies show the more hours of television children watch, the lower their verbal test scores will be. But what about adults? Colleagues at Emory University conducted a study to determine how reading a novel affected the brain compared to watching television. They chose the book *Pompeii* by Robert Harris for college students to read, since it has a dramatic plot based on true events—the eruption of Mount Vesuvius in Italy—and it has strong narration.

After the students read the novel, they "had increased connectivity in parts of the brain that were related to language. There was also increased activity in the sensory motor region of the brain, suggesting that readers experienced similar sensations to the characters in the book."[5]

Researchers also determined that reading tends to keep the mind alert and delays cognitive decline in older people. They even learned that Alzheimer's is two and a half times less likely to occur in older people who read regularly. Television watching, on the other hand, appears to be more of a risk factor.[6]

Understand how we filter our thoughts. Scientists tell us we have approximately sixty thousand thoughts in a day![7] That's more than one per every second we are awake. So how on earth can we possibly filter those so that we eliminate, for instance, all negative thoughts?

It is certain that you cannot avoid negative thoughts by consciously trying to eliminate them. If I tell you not to think of a pink elephant and to concentrate on eliminating all thoughts of a pink elephant from your mind, you will find that all you can think about is a pink elephant. But if you intentionally replace an unwanted thought with one you do want, you're more likely to experience the unwanted thought vanishing into the background. Dwelling on a positive replacement is a good way to filter out what you don't want.

Focusing our thoughts

Harvey Mackay learned an important lesson in focusing after he met Gary Player, the South African golfer, in 1955. They met on a practice round the day before the St. Paul Open. Player was an unknown professional golfer and Mackay was an unknown amateur who had won his varsity letter in golf at the University of Minnesota, and hadn't yet been talked out of playing professionally.

The two young men hit it off immediately. Mackay offered to show Player the sights and, along with half a dozen other young people, they had a great time. The next day, Mackay's tee-off time was in the afternoon and Player's was in the morning. Enthusiastic about his new friend, Mackay decided to walk with Player on his round.

After Player teed off on the first hole, Mackay reached him as he walked down the fairway. "Gary, how you doin' there?" he asked. "Didn't we have a great time last night?"

Player kept his eyes straight ahead, looking neither to the right or the left. It was as if he had blinders on. Finally he spoke: "Harvey, I can't talk to you. I must concentrate. I'll see you when I'm finished." Mackay was devastated.

Thirty years later, he ran into Player and his wife, and told them that story. Player's wife laughed and said, "Don't feel bad, Harvey. Actually, he was rather forthcoming with you. He won't even acknowledge my existence when he's on the golf course."[8]

Although it seems callous when you apply it to human relations, that kind of focus comes in handy when you're wanting to focus your thinking on the right words at the right time. Thinking the best thoughts will never become habitual if our focus is blurred, if our mind is racing all over the landscape.

Mark Victor Hansen said, "Focused mind power is one of the strongest forces on earth."[9] He should know; he has focused his mind power on writing *Chicken Soup for the Soul* books that have sold some 500 million copies throughout the world.

Ken Blanchard of *One Minute Manager* fame has written scores of books, believing that "human energy is like the energy of light. When it is dissipated, as in the average lightbulb, it gets work done in an average way. But when that same energy is focused and concentrated in a single direction, as with a laser beam, it has the power to cut through any kind of obstacle."[10]

So focus your thinking if you want to filter out the negative, unproductive words, and keep the words that inspire, motivate, and produce.

Prioritizing our thoughts

Did you hear about the man who went in search of a singing parakeet? As a bachelor, he felt his house was too quiet. In a pet store, the owner convinced him he had just the right bird for him, so the man bought it. When he came home from work the next day, the house was full of music. The parakeet sang beautifully.

When he went to the cage to feed the bird, he noticed for the first time that the parakeet had only one leg. He felt cheated. Why would the pet store owner sell him a one-legged bird? He called the store and complained.

"Well, what do you want," the owner responded, "a bird who can sing or a bird who can dance?"[11]

Life is made up of choices, by which we decide what's important to us. If we're going to prioritize our words on the way to thinking the best thoughts, we'll have to decide what is important. We'll have to learn to put first things first. C.S. Lewis said, "Put first things first and we get second things thrown in; put second things first and we lose both first and second things."[12]

Journalist Tim Redmond observed, "There are many things that will catch my eye, but there are only a few things that will catch my heart."[13]

How many times during the day do we find ourselves wasting time, shuffling papers, putting off decisions and projects until some later date, instead of concentrating on the things that really matter? Learning to prioritize and tackling first things first can become a habit if we work at it consistently. Filtering out the negative unproductive ideas, focusing on the things that matter, and learning to major on majors instead of frittering our time away on minor things will take us to the next level of prioritizing. This will lead us to thinking the best thoughts.

HEARING THE BEST IDEAS

Years ago a man went broke during the Great Depression. He didn't have a penny. However, he refused to surrender to the forces of depression. He kept his "ear to the ground," and he heard something inspiring.

A fellow salesman said, "Hey, did you hear about the guy who made so much money with Coca-Cola? You know, it used to be that the only way you could get a glass of soda was from a soda fountain. But then this guy came up with a way to bottle it. He told the Coca-Cola company that they could use his idea if they would give him a fraction of 1 percent of their increased sales. That minute percentage made him a millionaire."

When the man who was broke heard that story, it set him to thinking. That very day he had been to the gas station to get oil for his car. In those days, the only way to get oil was at the gas station where they pumped it out of huge drums and poured it into your car. He began to think, *I wonder if I could bottle oil?* But then it occurred to him that if a bottle of oil broke, it would create a big mess.

So he decided bottling oil was not a good idea, but why not put it in cans?

He visited a can company to see if they would sell him cans. He called on a friend in Pennsylvania who owned an oil well that produced more than he could market. Then he visited a grocery store chain and proposed a deal: if they would pay him seventy-five dollars for every freight car load of oil they sold, he could vastly increase their sales.

They were interested, so he arranged to sell them motor oil in cans. At seventy-five dollars per freight car of cans, he became a millionaire during the Great Depression.[14]

Great ideas are powerful. And valuable! But how can we put ourselves in a position to hear more great ideas?

Brainstorm to get more ideas

Brainstorming may seem commonplace to you, but it is not an ancient practice. In 1948, advertising executive Alex Osborne wrote a book, *Your Creative Power*, with a chapter on brainstorming. He defined it as "using the brain to storm a creative problem—and doing so in commando fashion, with each stormer attacking the same objective."[15]

Osborne offered four rules to guide groups in using the brainstorming technique:

1. No negative feedback. If people's ideas are shot down upon launch, they will soon clam up and refuse to share any more.

2. Focus on quantity over quality. There will be plenty of time to evaluate the best ideas over the average ones later. The plan in brainstorming is to generate as many as possible.

3. Use others' ideas as launchpads. Piggybacking on someone else's idea is perfectly acceptable. In fact, it is encouraged as a way to keep the creative juices flowing.

4. Encourage big thinking. No idea is too outlandish or oversized. Super-sized ideas can always be trimmed to more realistic standards later. During brainstorming, no judging is allowed. Just keep the ideas coming.

Almost everyone has had an experience of brainstorming with others. But what about brainstorming alone? Wait, isn't that an oxymoron? Some have discovered they produce even more ideas by brainstorming alone. Here are some strategies for solo brainstorming:[16]

Find word associations. For instance, choose a word that is unconnected to the topic of your brainstorming session. Suppose you are planning to set up a display at a conference that you hope will attract new customers. You think of a lightbulb, which has nothing to do with your display. But the lightbulb reminds you of the old flashbulbs photographers used, which generates the idea of a photographer who takes head shots of everyone who visits your booth.

Andy Kelund, a leadership trainer, also suggests a word association tool. For instance, the word *star* might also make you think of other words like *glitter, bright, sun, moon, sky, astronomy, twinkle, radiance,* and others. One of those words will get you to thinking about a creative idea that had not previously crossed your mind.

Use a prompt. You can buy packs of prompt cards that ask creative questions that start your thought processes in a new way. As an alternative, ask a coworker to make up a prompt. They don't even have to know what you're working on; they just need to ask a random question, such as, "Describe your challenge to someone in an elevator in ninety seconds."

Use a visual jumpstart. You can use Google Images to look for a photo that might be related to your subject. As you look at the photo, write down everything that comes to your mind. Then see if anything jumps out as a usable idea.

Give yourself boundaries. Although it seems counterintuitive, boundaries may force you to be more creative. The fewer resources you have, the more inventive you have to be. If you have three months to finish your task, ask yourself what you would do if you had only a day or a week.

Take away boundaries. Take away the fences and unleash the ideas. If you had an unlimited budget, what would you do? Obviously, your budget is not unlimited, so how can you turn that great idea into a more manageable one?

Just remember that to hear great ideas, you have to work at it. You may hear it from someone else. You may hear it in your own head as you brainstorm alone. As business philosopher Jim Rohn used to say, "If you wish to find, you must search. Rarely does a good idea interrupt you."[17]

Treat the ideas you hear with great care

How you treat people is an important concept. But so is how you treat ideas.

> Treat them tender…They can get killed pretty quickly.
>
> Treat them gently…They can be bruised in infancy.
>
> Treat them respectfully…They could be the most valuable things that ever came into your life.
>
> Treat them protectively…Don't let them get away.
>
> Treat them nutritionally…Feed them, and feed them well.
>
> Treat them antiseptically…Don't let them get infected with the germs of negative thoughts.
>
> Treat them responsibly! Respond! Do something with them![18]

Charles Browner would have agreed. He said, "A new idea is delicate. It can be killed by a sneer or a yawn; it can be stabbed to death by a quip and worried to death by a frown on the right man's brow."[19]

You do want to treat great ideas well. As Carl Schurz said, "Ideas are like stars; you will not succeed in touching them with your hands. But like the seafaring man on the desert of waters, you choose them as your guides, and following them you will reach your destiny."[20]

Having heard some great ideas, and having protected them and treated them well, how do we respond?

Respond to your ideas with action

I heard about an organization that offered one hundred dollars to a person who came up with an idea to cut costs. The first suggestion was: "Make the reward fifty dollars; that will cut costs."

It's a cynical reply, but you must admit, it's taking action on the idea. Not everyone takes action. Different people respond to ideas in different ways.

Insecure people hibernate. They may be afraid of failing or that it will take too much work. But either way, when winter blows its chilly breath in their direction, they rush off to hibernate and wait for warmer, more pleasant days.

Lazy people luxuriate. They have bought into the idea of enjoying life now and waiting until later to become serious.

Wounded people commiserate. Ever notice how people who have tried and failed love to commiserate with each other? Maybe it's the diets they tried, or the smoking they gave up dozens of times, or the drinking habit they abandoned only to take it up again.

Foolish people procrastinate. Putting it off is the most exercise some people ever get. The time isn't right, the weather isn't right, their mood isn't right—it's always something to prevent action now. So it never gets done.

Wise people dedicate. They don't let the grass grow under their feet. They get up and do it now. "They don't waste the most precious thing in the world—a good idea. They don't waste a good moment or a good opportunity."[21]

To say it even more succinctly, "Ideas without action are worthless."[22]

So no matter how many great ideas you hear—whether from group brainstorming, solo brainstorming, or some other source, you must treat them well and take decisive action or the ideas you hear will dissipate and come to nothing.

SPEAKING THE BEST WORDS

You have probably heard the story of the man who approached a judge about getting a divorce.

"Why do you want a divorce?" the judge asked. "On what grounds?"

"All over. We have an acre and a half," responded the man.

"No, no," said the judge. "Do you have a grudge?"

"Yes, sir. Fits two cars."

"I need a reason for the divorce," the judge said impatiently. "Does she beat you up?"

"Oh, no. I'm up at six every morning. She drags her carcass out of bed much later."

"Please," said the exasperated judge. "What is the reason for the divorce?"

"Oh, we can't seem to communicate with each other."

I hope your communication is several levels above that couple. But remember that filtering our words should help us speak the right words at the right time.

The right words at the right time

Mark Twain said, "The difference between the almost right word and the right word is…the difference between the lightning bug and the lightning."[23]

We all strive to find the right word at times because we know it may be the key to unlocking an important relationship. Harvey Mackay tells about visiting Cuba as part of the first delegation of businessmen to visit after Castro had taken power. Mackay had the rare privilege of a one-on-one with Castro. He spoke in English, and Castro, who supposedly spoke no English, spoke in Spanish. An interpreter provided translation.

Mackay said, "Comandante, I noticed you are in excellent physical condition. How did you do it?" Mackay already knew the dictator was athletic. He had read a biography that told him that before Castro got into politics, he was given a tryout as a pitcher by the old Washington Senators.

Mackay saw Castro's eyes light up *before* the translation. "Bowling," he said in Spanish. It turns out he had installed a bowling alley in the basement of the Palace of the Revolution. He reached into his breast pocket and pulled out a little notebook. It was where Castro kept a running tally of his scores and the results of his matches with his generals. The final column indicated who owed what to whom. And—no surprise—they all owed Castro. He had beaten them all.

Mackay said, "What an amazing coincidence. I happen to have won the University of Minnesota bowling championships three years in a row."

"Oh, you did?" Castro blurted—in English! In his excitement at finding a fellow bowler, all pretense of his inability to speak English had vanished.

The conversation quickly ended, but for a short time Mackay had succeeded in gaining an audience with a world leader, all because he knew something of Castro's background and used the right words at the right time to engage his interest.[24]

Most of us will never have the opportunity to interview a king, president, or dictator. But we do have the opportunity to talk with family members and coworkers.

Larry King, who reportedly interviewed some thirty thousand people in the twenty-five years he hosted *Larry King Live* on CNN, suggests some of the reasons why the best talkers are able to engage people so meaningfully.[25]

- *They look at things from a new angle.* Their subject may be familiar, but they take an unexpected point of view.

- *They have broad horizons.* You can find the right words if you think about and talk about a wide range of issues. But you need to move beyond your own daily life.

- *They are enthusiastic.* Almost everyone loves to engage with people who have a passion for what they are doing in their lives.

- *They don't talk about themselves all the time.* As British Prime Minister Benjamin Disraeli said, "Talk to a man about himself and he will listen for hours."[26]

- *They are curious.* They keep asking questions, not to be nosy, but because they really want to know more.

- *They empathize.* They are able to relate to others because they put themselves in their place.

- *They have a sense of humor.* They will even make themselves the butt of their jokes.

- *They have their own style of talking.* They're not afraid to be themselves.

What these pointers from Larry King tell us is that it's not only a matter of having a formula to find the right word at the right time. It's a matter of being yourself, being genuine, sincere, and truly caring about other people. When you have that going for you, you are more likely to find the right words at the right time.

The right words in the right way

How do you talk to people? Do you come across with arrogance? Brashness? Shyness? There are many ways to speak to people. Here is a little food for thought.

Try kindness. Some people seem to be naturally kind. And some definitely do not. Beth Walker tells about Dan, whose daughter Kristen asked her mother, Ann, one day, "Who is that man? One minute he's hollering at me because my room is a mess, and the next, he's on the phone as nice as can be to someone he hardly knows."

People who haven't learned to treat others with kindness have the power to crush the spirits of their family members. Author and counselor Gary Smalley calls it "closing the spirit." It tends to stifle communication and closeness.

Kristen admitted, "When my dad yells, I don't want to do anything he asks. When he's polite, I feel like pleasing him."

Ann says, "When I screw up and my husband responds kindly instead of reacting harshly, I fall in love all over again."

Kindness can make the difference. It's sad when a person uses up all their niceness on their secretaries and clients and gives the leftovers to their family members.[27]

Try firmness. A friend told me how difficult it was to let a subordinate go. The man had a family, which should always make you think twice about terminating someone. But the man had lost credibility. He had been unwise. He had said too much in mixed company. For instance, he was too graphic about the process of his wife giving birth. He didn't filter his words as he should have. He had shown enough insensitivity that the people around him were gun-shy. They never knew what he was going to say next. People felt uneasy around him. It was bad for business.

So my friend had to let him go. "You have great ability," he told the man. "You have good skills. I can give you a good recommendation.

If you will profit from your mistakes and start over somewhere else, I believe you can still be productive and successful."

It was hard, but sometimes we have to talk to people with firmness. We don't have to be cruel. We don't have to insult or demean. But we have to be honest, tell it like it is, and endeavor to make the best of a difficult situation.

The right words for the right reason

Why do you want to say the right words in the right way? What is your motivation? Sometimes we want to inform. Other times we may want our words to heal. A worthy goal for every conversation is to be sure our words help.

Informing. Teachers inform. Colleagues inform. Doctors inform. Some are better at it than others. Alistair Cooke once said, "Suppose that a first-rate teacher of the English language gave regular courses to medical students during their internship—or, better, that there was always someone on hand to translate into English the parts and functions of the body at the moment a student was learning them...then the day might even come when doctors would talk to patients about collar-bones instead of clavicles."[28]

To inform, we must know what we want to say and how to say it in the best way to communicate the information we're trying to get across to someone else. If the house is on fire, we don't want to think too long about how we fashion our speech to let people know. But on less urgent matters, it's best if we speak clearly and with confidence.

Healing. Sometimes our words can heal. Saying, "I am sorry," when we know we have offended someone certainly aids in the healing process. Some people contend that those three words—*I am sorry*—are the most healing words we can say.

Think of the emotional healing that comes when an abusive parent finally comes to the point when he or she can say, "I am sorry," and mean it. It doesn't undo the pain of the past, but it can begin the healing process.

Imagine saying "I am sorry" to a coworker after retelling a story about that coworker and later learning that the story was untrue and unfounded. When words of regret are expressed sincerely, it can begin to mend a fractured relationship.

Some people say, "Sorry," with a roll of the eyes, and you can tell it is not sincere. But said with conviction and heartfelt pain for the hurt that has been caused will make a crucial difference.

Filtering words is not a walk in the park. It means training ourselves to think the best thoughts, hear the best ideas, and speak the right words. As we work on those challenges, with an emphasis on thinking, hearing, and speaking what is true and helpful, we will discover that our words have power—incredible, life-changing power.

Chapter Five

BLESSING OTHERS

To bless someone or something is to wish good for it. Likewise, the opposite is to curse, or to wish the worst. Jesus said, "Whatever is in your heart determines what you say" (Matthew 12:34 NLT). This chapter will show you how to speak words of blessing, both upon yourself and others, by examining the intentions of your heart.

"Be true to yourself, help others, make each day your masterpiece, make friendship a fine art, drink deeply from good books—especially the Bible, build a shelter against a rainy day, give thanks for your blessings and pray for guidance every day."

JOHN WOODEN[1]

The idea of blessing has an interesting origin. To find it, we have to go back to the Germanic people of northern Germany and southern Scandinavia, where ancient people sprinkled blood on pagan altars. It later came to mean "hallow with blood" or "mark with blood." When the Old English adopted the word, it meant "to consecrate by a religious rite, to make holy, give thanks."

When the Old English were looking for a word to translate certain thoughts from the Greek and Hebrew, they used this word to mean "to speak well of, to praise." Its meaning later shifted toward "pronounce or make happy, prosperous, or fortunate."[2]

In whatever way you have thought of the word before, I want to challenge you to think of blessing others as a way to wish them happiness, prosperity, and good fortune. To want only the best for others is a goal toward which we legitimately aspire.

I heard about a group of friends who had trained themselves to think of others by using *bless* as an acrostic. When they wanted to "bless others," they thought of it this way:

Body (health and strength)
Labor (work, security)
Emotional (joy, peace, hope)
Social (love, marriage, family and friends)
Spiritual (faith, relationship with God)

BLESSINGS FOR THE BODY

What is it we are really saying when someone sneezes and we say, "Bless you!"? I think we're really saying, "I hope you have good health. I hope that sneeze is not an indication that you're catching a cold. May whatever caused it be temporary and may you feel well and do well."

When we get the news that someone has cancer, our hearts sink because we wish them well. We hate to think they're going to have to face chemotherapy, radiation, loss of hair, and all the other side effects that go along with many cancer treatments. When we hear someone has some other debilitating condition, we cringe. We know their lives are going to be affected, usually in adverse ways. We don't like to think of ourselves or others having to face the physical limitations that go along with certain conditions.

We wish for ourselves and all our friends good health and sufficient strength to keep up a normal lifestyle. We don't like to think of ourselves as limited by physical conditions that slow us down or cause us inconvenience.

Dealing with physical limitations

We're always impressed when we hear of people who face physical limitations but manage to rise above them with a great attitude and a sense of humor. I think of Nick Vujicic, who was born without arms or legs.

When Nicholas Vujicic (pronounced VOO-yee-cheech) was born in 1982 in Melbourne, Australia, nothing prepared his parents for the fact that he had no arms or legs. Sonograms had not indicated they should expect any complications or birth defects. As you can imagine, during his childhood and adolescence, he struggled with depression and loneliness. He wondered why he was different from other kids and whether he had a purpose.

He credits his faith in God, his family, and his friends with enabling him to gain victory over his struggles. He travels around the world, sharing his story and providing inspiration to various groups of people. He sometimes speaks to stadiums filled with people. Sometimes he speaks to small groups of teachers, students, business people, and church congregations of all sizes.[3]

Nick has so thoroughly triumphed over his limitations that he is able to joke about them. At one venue, the crowd was so large and the space so limited they had to turn away five hundred people. Not wanting to limit the size of his crowd, he looked into renting the Staple Center in Los Angeles. He said, "That would cost an arm and a leg. And I don't have that!"[4]

It takes an incredibly positive attitude to see blessings in the absence of arms and legs.

Daily strength

Most of us have arms and legs. The question is: what do we do with them daily that makes us a blessing to others? Henry Ward Beecher, clergyman and social reformer well-known for his support of the abolition of slavery, said, "Greatness lies not in being strong, but in the right use of strength."[5]

Young people stereotypically like to boast about their strength. One young man who worked on a construction site kept bragging that he could outdo anyone in a test of strength, and he especially taunted the older workers on the job.

Finally, one of the older men had heard enough. He calmly stepped up to the young man and said, "Put your money where your mouth is." He pointed across the construction site and said, "I'll bet you a week's

wages that I can haul something over to that building in a wheelbarrow that you can't haul back."

"You're on, old man," the braggart replied. "Now let's see what
you've got."

The older man grabbed the handles of a wheelbarrow. Nodding to
the young man, he said, "All right, get in."[6]

Clever! But strength is not all about size and bulging muscles. Think
of the hummingbird. It darts from one flower to the next almost faster
than the eye can follow. I have read that if human beings exerted as
much energy as a hummingbird, we would have to eat between two
hundred and four hundred pounds a day just to maintain that energy!
Fortunately, we can get by on far less than that.

The fact is that God, who created both hummingbirds and human
beings, gives each of us the amount of strength we need to do all that
he wants us to do.[7]

You may have had days when you questioned that statement. All
the strength we need? Really? Can you single out one day when life was
so difficult, you wondered if you would make it?

If you're reading this, of course, you made it. Somehow you found
the strength, the energy, the resolve, the determination to put one foot
in front of another and complete each day.

Moses led the people of Israel for forty years—one day at a time. I
imagine there were days when he wondered if he would make it. Imagine confronting Pharaoh, arguably the most powerful man in the world
at that time. Imagine demanding that he let your people, the Hebrews
who had been enslaved to Egypt for something like four hundred years,
leave Egypt and go back to their Promised Land in Canaan. Moses
probably shivered in his sandals and wondered if he would make it
through that day.

Imagine facing the waters of the Red Sea ahead of you and the
advancing Egyptian army behind you. How do you find the courage to
stand and tell the people to hold steady and watch God work? How do
you find the courage to stretch out your arm and let the Lord open the
way by rolling back the water so the people can walk through on dry
ground? I daresay Moses wondered if he would make it through that day.

Moses had some long days, especially when the food and water ran out, and the people criticized him, blaming him for luring them out of Egypt only to be stranded in the desert. Where did he get the strength to press on, in spite of the criticism?

When he came near to the end of his life, Moses named each tribe of Israel and spoke a blessing over the people of that tribe. I especially like what he told the tribe of Asher: "The bolts of your gates will be iron and bronze," he told them, "and your strength will equal your days" (Deuteronomy 33:25). Some readers may remember the King James Version: "As thy days, so shall thy strength be." Either way you say it, Moses believed God was the source of our strength and the one who can help us face every day.

When we say to others, "Have a good day," I hope we are wishing them the health, strength, energy, and stamina for each day.

BLESSINGS FOR OUR LABOR

Mia Hamm is a retired professional soccer player, two-time Olympic gold medalist, and two-time FIFA Women's World Cup champion. She played as a forward for the United States women's national soccer team from 1987–2004. As a college student at the University of North Carolina, she played for the Tar Heels women's soccer team and helped them win four consecutive NCAA Division I Women's Soccer Championship titles.[8]

In college the players had to meet individually with their coach and tell him what goals they were shooting for each semester. The players decided their goals, and the coach helped them plan a way to achieve them. The meetings were serious. This wasn't just a meaningless exercise.

Mia wanted the goals to be ambitious enough to be challenging, but realistic enough to be attainable. She says her coach, Anson Dorrance, was a great coach—supportive, encouraging, and motivating. She described him as being direct and no-nonsense. He would know when a student was faking it. For some reason, in her sophomore year, she couldn't identify what she wanted to do next. Against her better judgment, she went into the meeting with the coach unprepared. She was scared.

When they sat down, one on either side of his cluttered desk, he waited for Mia to speak. She expressed uncertainty and danced around the topic. He listened patiently, nodded occasionally, and waited for her to stop rambling. Finally, he leaned forward and said, "What do you want?"

She blurted, "To be the best."

Be your best

As soon as she said it, she couldn't believe it. It seemed totally absurd. But she added, "This semester, one of my goals is to be the best."

He sat there a moment and said, "Do you know what the best is?"

She thought about it. She began telling herself it was a fantasy, something she had only thought about in the abstract. She didn't know what it meant. She started to sweat and avoided eye contact.

The coach stood up and walked around the desk to the light switch on the wall behind her. He turned the light off and for one second, they were in darkness. Then he switched the light back on. "It's just a decision," he said. "But you have to make it every day."

He was telling her she had to choose between mediocrity and excellence every time she woke up. If she reached for her best, she had to work that hard to catch up to her dreams. Being the best, she discovered, is not glamorous. It's not about glory or talent. She learned it is about commitment, doing incredibly hard work. She came to understand it means you can't ever live with "good enough." It's discouraging at times and almost always exhausting. But unless she committed herself to it every day, she didn't get the results she wanted to achieve.[9]

Playing soccer was Mia Hamm's work. It was her labor. Her coach's words proved to be a blessing because they helped to motivate her to do her best. She is ranked number two among the greatest female soccer players of all time.[10]

Cleaning up

Labor can be extremely competitive as one budding entrepreneur discovered when she opened a cleaning business in a small city. She became aware of the reputation of one wealthy woman who never used any cleaning service more than once. She had a large home and expected those who cleaned it to give good service, but she never hired the same service twice.

When the entrepreneur got the call to clean for this woman, she was determined to give it her very best. As she and her employees cleaned the house, they found loose change along the way. They placed it in a little cup in the kitchen.

Upon completion of the work, the woman paid her and she left.

A few weeks later, she was shocked when the wealthy woman called and asked her to clean her house a second time. She could not believe it when no one else had been given that opportunity.

She told the woman she would love to clean her house again, but she had to ask why she was getting another opportunity.

> "It's very simple," the wealthy woman told her. "One dollar and sixty-one cents."

> "Excuse me?"

> "You were the only one who found the entire $1.61 in change that I had strategically placed throughout the house," she explained. "Some people found eighty-nine cents. Some found ninety. Some found $1.25. One found $1.40. But you were the only one who found the entire $1.61."[11]

Hard work, excellent work, diligent work, accompanied by honesty, is a blessing.

Have you ever studied the ant? Maybe as a kid you watched ants crawling around your yard. If you put a stick in their path, no problem; they climb over it. If you put a rock in their way, no sweat; they walk around it. Whatever you do to hinder an ant, it will simply keep moving over it or around it. Or he may get some buddies to help him move it out of the way. What do ants do to get the job done? Whatever it takes!

The ancient wise man pointed out the ant's ability to plan ahead. He said the ant "stores its provisions in summer and gathers its food at harvest" (Proverbs 6:8). While we human beings must labor and sweat to carry out the law of sowing and reaping, the ant instinctively under-stands the law of storing and gathering.

We would be wise to imitate the ant, both in its industrious nature and in its ability to plan ahead, providing for the future.

The person who is willing to work hard is in demand. Andrew Carnegie observed, "The average person puts 25 percent of his energy and ability into his work. The world takes off its hat to those who put in more than 50 percent of their capacity, and stands on its head for those few and far between souls who devote 100 percent."[12]

If someone has blessed you with a job, you are fortunate. As you give that job your best, you are being a blessing to others.

BLESSINGS FOR THE EMOTIONS

Business philosopher Jim Rohn said, "Our emotions need to be as educated as our intellect. It is important to know how to feel, how to respond, and how to let life in so that it can touch you."[13]

A little help

It was the young man's first flight and he was obviously nervous. When he found his seat, he fidgeted, his eyes darting back and forth to the aircraft windows. He tried various means of calming himself—closing his eyes, breathing deeply, rocking back and forth on take-off.

An older woman sitting across the aisle from him reached over and put her hand on his arm. She engaged him in conversation, doing her best to divert his mind from the stress. She asked him his name, where he was from. She gave assurances like, "We're going to be okay" and "You're doing well."

When the young man sat down, she had a choice to make. She could have been irritated with him. She could have ignored him. Instead she chose to touch him and say a few words. And it made a positive difference. Three hours later, when they landed, he thanked her for helping him.[14]

The young man was fortunate to have a caring person seated near him. She saw his need and intervened. For those who are not so for-tunate to have a handy helper nearby, it's important to realize we can actually choose which emotions will govern our day.

You choose

Bill Vossler proposes the hypothetical situation in which two men are driving to work. A beautiful new red sports car cuts in front of Dan, narrowly missing his front bumper. Dan becomes furious. His blood pressure rises, he can feel his heart thumping in his chest, he gives vent to a string of obscenities, and smacks the steering wheel. The rest of the day, he fumes and mutters about the jerk who cut him off.

Dave has the same experience; the same red sports car cuts him off too. He is momentarily irked. But then he waves and says to himself that it really doesn't matter if the other guy gets ahead of him. So instead of fuming, he whistles the rest of the way to work.

Dan's and Dave's experiences look the same on the surface, but Dan chose to prolong his anger. Dave didn't.[15]

A motivational speaker once spoke on the topic: "Make up your mind before you make up your bed." In other words, before you leave your bedroom, decide what kind of day you're going to have. Don't be controlled by the whims of the day. Determine in advance that you will choose cheerfulness and a positive attitude to be your companions throughout the day.

It's one thing to choose to have a good attitude when a red sports car cuts you off, but what if something vastly more important happens. Penelope Russianoff, a clinical psychologist, reflected on the death of her husband, a world-renowned musician and teacher. They had a loving marriage, and the emotional pain from losing someone that close can be devastating. However, she chose to concentrate on the twenty-four years of happiness they shared. She chose to focus on the emotional blessings instead of the emotional loss.

She even went so far as to say, "We create our own emotional environment, with our families, on the job, and among our friends, by the way we look at things." She continued, "We can create a negative environment and wallow in it, or we can create a positive environment and succeed in it."[16]

One man complains, "My life is so lousy, I'm talking to myself." But there is a positive self-talk that can work to your advantage. It's actually "one of the best ways to change how you feel. Simple as it sounds, it is one of the most effective techniques you can use for breaking negative habits."[17]

As Vossler observes, "You are a magician. You can conjure whatever mood you want, whenever you want." And Russianoff adds, "The door to changing our feelings is always open. We just have to choose to walk through it."[18]

Emotional problems are complex, and saying you can talk yourself out of them may sound like too simple a way to deal with them. However, thoughts and feelings are intermingled. If we can train ourselves to change the way we think, we may just change the way we feel. And what a blessing that would be!

BLESSINGS FOR OUR SOCIAL RELATIONSHIPS

Among the blessings we enjoy in our social relationships, family and friends are two of the most cherished.

Family

In her book, *Reflections: Life After the White House*, Barbara Bush told about the summer of 1999 when all of her and George H.W. Bush's children came to Kennebunkport. She remembered that one week a team of George W.'s advisers showed up to brief him. George W. was governor of Texas at the time, and the *Washington Post* had run seven articles on him. She thought all seven had been fair. One said, "He comes out as a nice guy who is decent and honest…not perfect, but a really good person."

Remembering that sparked the memory of going to church one Sunday. The minister that day asked the congregation if anyone had a perfect family. He was talking about "the family of man" and used the idea of the human family to make a point. Mrs. Bush recalled that everyone in her family sat on their hands, "which, I guess is what he expected, probably hoped for. But one hand did go up and it was George Bush's [her husband]. The minister made a little fun of that and I heard a quiet George say: 'To me they seem almost perfect.' We all felt badly that we hadn't raised our hands, and I certainly felt a tear coming. George Bush is the sweetest man."[19]

We can forgive Mrs. Bush for her bias toward her family, but the most skeptical among us would have to admit, watching her funeral in April 2018, we could not help but be impressed with the close-knit nature of the Bush family.

Jon Meacham, a presidential historian, said Mr. Bush had told him, concerning Mrs. Bush, "She's the rock of the family, the leader of the family. I kind of float above it all."[20]

When we think of social blessing, having a close-knit family is one of the greatest advantages we can imagine. Every time we give a wedding card to a bride and groom on their wedding day, we are saying, "May you and your family be richly blessed." Every time we congratulate a couple on the birth of a child, we are saying, "Wow! Your family is so blessed with this beautiful new life." Even when a close loved one passes away, whatever we say or do to support the family, we are expressing our sympathy at this loss of blessing from their family unit.

Friends

Friendship is another social blessing. The rhinoceros prowls the grasslands of East Africa. Its tremendous size, speed, and agility make it one of the most feared animals in the region. Most other creatures avoid it.

However, the buffalo bird perches on its back. It flies around the rhino's head, lands on its ears, and pecks away. Yet the rhino never attacks because the two have an understanding. The rhino has poor eyesight. Its body is covered with parasites that the rhino is helpless to control. The buffalo bird eats the parasites. It also lets out a shrill call to warn of any danger. Although the two animals are quite different from each other, they have an understanding, a friendship of sorts.[21]

Jackie Robinson, the first black man to play major league baseball, and Pee Wee Reese were quite different from each other. Jackie Robinson faced hostile crowds in nearly every stadium in the early days of his career. He played for the Brooklyn Dodgers and one day, playing in his home stadium, he made an error. The fans—the Dodger fans—began booing him mercilessly. He stood there, devastated, while the fans kept on jeering and throwing insults.

Then Pee Wee Reese, who played shortstop, ran over and put his arm around Jackie's shoulder. Gradually, the fans quieted down. They could hardly believe the two men, one black and one white, stood there side-by-side. Jackie later admitted that he wondered if his career would have been over had it not been for Pee Wee Reese's friendship.[22]

Dr. James Lynch cites statistics that show the death rate for adults without deep relationships is twice that of people who enjoy regular caring interaction with others. In our culture, many people are almost obsessive over their health, monitoring cholesterol intake and calorie consumption, but ignore their relational life. Scientists tell us that our relational lives have just as much impact on our physical health as things like smoking, high blood pressure, and lack of exercise.[23]

C.S. Lewis, in his characteristically graphic way, bemoaned our tendency to treat friendship as a side dish rather than "a main course in life's banquet." He says the result, for many, has become "emotional malnutrition."[24]

Ted Engstrom tells about a young man he met in Calcutta. The boy, a fifteen-year-old named Dwarka Das, tugged at Ted's trouser leg and asked him if he wanted a shoeshine. It was late and Ted was tired. Looking at his watch, he said, "Perhaps tomorrow."

When he left the hotel six hours later, the shoeshine boy was still there, offering "the best shoeshine in Calcutta." As he shined, they talked and became friends. Over the next several days, Ted had more shoeshines in one week than ever before. One day, Dwarka Das gave Ted a photo of himself and signed it, "From your friend in Calcutta." Ted gave him a Polaroid picture of himself, and they began to correspond.

Eighteen months later, Ted returned to Calcutta, only to find flowers in his room, compliments of Dwarka Das, who somehow learned of his arrival. Once again, Ted treated himself to more shoeshines than his shoes needed. And their correspondence continued.

One day Ted received a long letter from his young friend, who said in the last sentence, "Mr. Ted, you give me many things. Books, letters, good tips for shoeshine. But one thing most good you give me is you are my friend. Thank you, Mr. Ted, for you be my friend."[25]

BLESSINGS FOR THE SPIRITUAL

In the autumn of 1992, Michael Plant set out to sail across the Atlantic Ocean. His planned route would take him from the United States through the North Atlantic to France. Two weeks into the voyage, he and his sailboat were lost at sea. It should never have happened.

Plant was an expert yachtsman, held in high esteem by the sailing community. His sailboat, the *Coyote*, was state of the art. Its design, its features, its comforts were top-notch.

Plant also purchased a new emergency radio beacon. With four short signal-bursts to a satellite, he could enable ground stations to determine his exact location.

However, something went wrong. Eleven days into the voyage, radio contacts in America stopped receiving his messages. After several days of silence, they became suspicious.

Rescue aircraft began looking for Plant's boat. For days, they saw and heard nothing. Then the crew of a freighter found the *Coyote*, 450 miles northwest of the Azores islands. There was no sign of Michael Plant, and his boat was upside down. Unheard of for a sailboat.

Sailboats, according to people who know, do not capsize. Usually, sailboats will right themselves even if wind and waves momentarily push them over or even upside down. The reason sailboats do not capsize is that they are built with more weight below the waterline than above it. To violate this principle is to invite disaster. The *Coyote* was built with a four-ton weight bolted to its keel. When the boat was found, the weight was missing.[26]

Below the waterline

That's a parable for you and me. What people see of our lives is, figuratively, above the waterline. The spiritual dimension within all of us is below the waterline. We work hard at being sure what people see looks good. We tend to neglect what they don't see—the spiritual. But when the storms of life come, if we have too little weight below the waterline, we capsize.

So to stay upright, to sail through life coping well with all the storms and high waves that come our way, we need a significant spiritual weight below the waterline. To seek to improve our spiritual dimension and to encourage the same in others results in blessing both for them and us.

I mentioned Nick Vujicic earlier in this chapter. He is a man of strong faith in God and his spiritual dimension is well-grounded. He bears no hostility toward God for the fact that he was born without appendages. He believes in prayer, although prayer has not grown a new set of limbs for him. Instead he has decided to use what he does have—a voice and a positive attitude of faith—to inspire others instead of railing against the universe.

Prayer

Clay Routledge, a professor and psychological scientist, writing in *National Review Online*, points to "the tested psychological and social benefits of prayer as well as the reality of how most believers turn to faith-based practices in addition to, not instead of, other courses of action."[27]

How is prayer a blessing? One study of older adults shows that the negative effects of financial problems on one's health were significantly reduced for people who pray regularly for others. Prayer has psychological benefits for those who think of God as loving instead of as distant and unresponsive. When people's prayers centered on gratitude and care for others, the people who prayed had the fewest symptoms of depression. All of this seems to say that prayer is good medicine.

Routledge is not suggesting people who pray have less faith in science or medical treatment. He says, "For most believers, prayer isn't a substitute for data-based solutions. It is a personal resource that complements and may even help facilitate other thoughtful action."[28]

William Wilberforce, a British politician, philanthropist, and leader of a movement to stop the slave trade, was also a man of prayer. His prayer fueled his faith in God and constrained him to act on behalf of his fellow man.[29] Because he cared deeply about the health and well-being of others, he supported the campaign for the complete abolition of slavery. It took many years of diligent service to see his cause come to fruition. Although he resigned from Parliament in 1826 due to his own failing health, he continued to campaign against slavery. Slavery was finally abolished in most of the British Empire in 1833 with the Slavery Abolition Act, passed by Parliament just three days before Wilberforce died.[30]

Examination

American poet Mary Oliver believes the instructions for living are three simple statements: "Pay attention. Be astonished. Tell about it."[31]

That's not a bad approach to examining your own spiritual development. Are you paying attention to what is happening in your life? Are your circumstances helping you grow or driving you farther away from God? What have you been learning on your life journey? What have your failures taught you? Who are the people who have spoken into your life, either intentionally or unintentionally, through books or other media?

What level of astonishment do you have about life? Do you see God's hand in any of the activities you have experienced? The books you have read? The movies you have seen? The people you have met? David Benner says, "Our challenge is to unmask the divine in the natural and name the presence of God in our lives."[32]

How are you telling the story about what you are observing? Sibyl Towner suggests we do this by helping others to pay attention, to be astonished by God's activity in their everyday lives, and by encouraging them to tell it to others.[33]

In a chapter about blessing others, I would be remiss if I did not bring to mind one of the outstanding Scriptures in this regard. God spoke to Abraham and said,

> I will make you into a great nation,
>   and I will bless you;
> I will make your name great,
>   and you will be a blessing.
> I will bless those who bless you,
>   and whoever curses you I will curse;

and all the peoples on earth
will be blessed through you
(Genesis 12:2-3).

Okay, so you're not Abraham. Neither am I. But I do believe God wants to bless each of us and make us a blessing to others. It's one of the privileges we have: blessing others.

Chapter Six

TRUTH TELLING

Truth is the basic power behind words, so it's vital to
ensure that your words are truthful. What are some
subtle forms of untruth that can creep into your speech?
How can we better harness the incredible power of
telling the truth, gracefully, in all situations?

*"Truth is always strong, no matter how weak it looks; and
falsehood is always weak, no matter how strong it looks."*
PHILLIPS BROOKS[1]

Five years after he graduated from college, American media personality Phil Donahue was working for WHIO radio and television in Dayton, Ohio. He and his cameraman had been dispatched to a mountain in West Virginia to cover a mine collapse that had trapped thirty-eight men underground. He was also doing radio reports for CBS News out of New York. That was the era when Edward R. Murrow and Walter Cronkite were big names at CBS. Although he was only on radio, Donahue took great pride that he was reporting for the same network.

Every night he phoned in his reports to both New York and Dayton on the tragedy that was occurring in the snows of Holden, West Virginia. Anxious family members gathered at the entrance to the doomed mine and Donahue reported about what a tough breed miners were. He could imagine his voice traveling out over the airwaves and into farmhouses, urban high-rises, and taverns throughout the free world.

One day as the miners took a break from their rescue efforts, they gathered around an old barrel filled with burning scrap wood. A thirty-something preacher prayed a spontaneous prayer: "Dear God, we ask your blessing at this troubled time..."

Donahue says it was a classic scene. The preacher was surrounded by the sooty faces of miners whose lamp-caps framed their working-men's features. As he finished his prayer, the miners began to sing,

> What a friend we have in Jesus.
> All our sins and griefs to bear;
> What a privilege to carry
> Everything to God in prayer.

And the preacher said, "Bless us, Lord, hold us in your arms."

Donahue said it was profoundly beautiful and inspiring. The rock-solid faith of mountain folk, the fearful eyes of the women and children, the snow falling from heaven, and a Protestant hymn he had never heard sung at a Catholic mass. They touched his heart, he said.

But panic set in because the camera made a grinding sound. In the freezing temperatures it had frozen up in some way. Donahue stood there, helpless. They had missed this beautiful, classic moment. No film, no feature, no world fame for this fledgling reporter, covering a heartrending tragedy.

They moved the camera closer to the fire in the barrel, stroked it, and offered their own prayer for its recovery. It finally revived and Donahue made his move. He approached the minister and began, "Reverend, I'm Phil Donahue from CBS News. We had some camera problems and were not able to record your wonderful prayer. Our equipment is ready now; may I ask you to repeat that prayer and I will ask the miners to sing again."

The preacher looked troubled. "But I have already prayed, son," he said.

"Reverend," Phil persisted, "I am from CEE BEE ESS NEWS." Donahue was impressed whether the preacher was or not.

"But I have already prayed," he repeated. "It wouldn't be right to pray again. Wouldn't be honest."

"But, Reverend, your prayer will appear on more than two hundred television stations of CBS News. Millions of people will see and hear your prayer and join you in petitioning God's help for these trapped miners. You will be seen by millions of viewers throughout the free world, demonstrating the deep religious faith of West Virginians and reminding viewers everywhere that God is good." Donahue was almost begging, because it would get him, the reporter, on national television.

"No," said the preacher. "It wouldn't be right. I have already prayed to my God." Then he turned and walked away, leaving CBS News standing in the snow.

Donahue said it was months later before it hit him. The preacher demonstrated more courage than he had ever seen in his lifetime. In a world of posturing and religious pomp, here was a man of God who refused to perform for television. His prayer had already been offered and repeating it would have been phony. "It wouldn't be right," the preacher had said.

Donahue said, "No matter my pleadings, he would not do 'take two' for Jesus. Not for me, not for all those taverns, not for 'millions of people throughout the free world.' Not even, praise the Lord, for CEE BEE ESS NEWS."[2]

How different from so much of our culture. *Time* magazine once devoted a cover article to the subject of lying. In a clever twist, the cover showed a man in dark glasses, and on one lens was the word "LYING" in capital letters. On the other were the words, "Everybody's doin' it (Honest)." The article concluded, "Lies flourish in social uncertainty when people no longer understand, or agree on, the rules governing their behavior toward one another. During such periods skepticism also increases; there will be the perception that more people are lying, whether or not they actually are."[3]

Clinical psychologist David J. Ley says, "People, by and large, are honest by default. Most people tell the truth most of the time. Our very capacity for language is built on an assumption of honesty—we agree that the words we use mean the same thing consistently, and we don't use words deceptively because this would render language and the very communication of ideas impossible."[4]

So for our world to continue revolving, we need to be able to trust people to be truthful. Yet people do lie.

Maybe you have heard about the minister who told his congregation, "Next week I plan to preach about the sin of lying. To help you understand my sermon, I want you all to read Mark 17."

The following Sunday, as he prepared to deliver his sermon, the minister asked for a show of hands. He wanted to know how many had read Mark 17.

Every hand went up.

The minister smiled and said, "Mark only has sixteen chapters. I will now proceed with my sermon on the sin of lying."

Do you know a lie is more trouble than telling the truth? Often a lie expands people's problems instead of getting them off the hook.

Take the guy in Sheboygan, Wisconsin, who accumulated a bunch of unpaid traffic tickets. During a routine traffic stop, this man, who wasn't even driving the car, gave a fictitious name to police because he wanted to hide the fact that he had a number of unpaid tickets.

When the police ran the fictitious name through their computers, they came up with some bad news. The real person whose name he gave was wanted for vehicular homicide. Who knew?

When he tried to deny the fake name, police released him only after fingerprints and photographs proved he was not the wanted man.[5]

Several years ago, Oprah Winfrey made a selection for her book club that turned out to be a fabrication. A novel, which everyone knows is fictional, is one thing, but a memoir that turns out to be untrue is something else.

Among other things, the author, James Frey, in his book *A Million Little Pieces*, claimed he hit a police officer with his car, fought the arresting officers, and spent three months in jail. Actually, police arrested him for drunk driving, no fighting occurred, he didn't hit anyone with his car, and he spent about five hours in jail.

He later labeled his writing "subjectivity." In other words, he claimed it was a personal recounting of a story instead of a precise reproduction of facts.[6]

Why do we want to embellish the truth? Why are we reluctant to let the facts speak for themselves?

One answer comes, not from a religious prophet, but from a television newsman. Ted Koppel says, "Our society finds Truth too strong a medicine to digest undiluted. In its purest form Truth is not a polite tap on the shoulder; it is a howling reproach. What Moses brought down from Mount Sinai were not the Ten Suggestions…They are Commandments. Are, not were."[7]

Since I brought up religious prophets, let me quote from the ancient wise man: "Truthful lips endure forever, but a lying tongue lasts only a moment" (Proverbs 12:19).

SEVEN LEVELS OF LYING

Sarah Sumner suggests seven levels of lying. She credits J. Budziszewski, author of *What We Can't Know*, with originating the idea of "seven degrees of descent," which she adapts into the seven levels.[8]

1. You lie

A simple lie, Sumner contends, can blaze into a bonfire. It reminds us of what James said, "Consider what a great forest is set on fire by a small spark. The tongue also is a fire, a world of evil among the parts of the body. It corrupts the whole body, sets the whole course of one's life on fire" (James 3:5-6). If a person refuses to confess the truth about a lie, he or she is on the way to level 2.

We may rationalize that it's only a "little white lie." Melissa Carver points out that many people say they're fine when they really are not. They may say they like someone's hair when they truthfully do not like it. "These lies build up," she says, "one on top of another. Once we tell ourselves these lies are harmless, telling larger lies becomes easier."[9] As someone said, "It is easy to tell one lie but difficult to tell only one."

2. You self-protect

In other words, people lie about having lied. Budziszewski says, "Lies are weaklings; they need bodyguards."

We may be trying to protect ourselves from embarrassment if the truth were known. We may be afraid others would be judgmental if they knew the truth about us. Children are often afraid of being punished if their parents find out the truth. Adults may fear the loss of others' respect. Obviously, there are many reasons why people lie to protect themselves from all manner of unwanted attention or unpleasant results.

3. You develop a habit of lying

When people arrive at this level, they may lie about something trivial, even when it appears they receive no benefit, because they have developed the habit of lying.

Carole Spiers suggests that lying may become a habit because we learned as children that we could avoid punishment by lying. Or people may have learned they could get their own way if they lied. Of course, this leads to stress as people struggle to remember exactly what they said to whom. Which story did they tell to which person?[10]

As Mark Twain said, "If you tell the truth, you don't have to remember anything."[11]

4. You self-deceive

It's possible to deceive oneself because now we begin to believe our own lies. People have a tremendous capacity for self-deception. The ancient prophet said, "The heart is deceitful above all things and beyond cure. Who can understand it?" (Jeremiah 17:9).

David J. Ley believes some people lie because telling the truth feels like they are giving up control. He says, "Often, people tell lies because they are trying to control a situation and exert influence toward getting the decisions or reactions they want."[12] However, this is a form of self-deception because eventually the truth will come out and the person who lies will both lose face and lose control.

5. You rationalize

People reach this level when they begin to justify their lies as positive good. They tell themselves it will help the company grow or save jobs. Sumner points out this type of thinking contributed to scandals at Enron and WorldCom.

Sumner admits this type of lying can be especially dangerous for a person climbing the corporate ladder. It's easy to think the lie is justified on the basis of being best for the institution. Or an adulterer convinces himself that what he is experiencing is love, not adultery. He rationalizes his marriage was just a convenience for the sake of bearing and rearing children. It can't compare with the "true love" he has now found.

6. You develop your technique

Sumner suggests the main technique is to compartmentalize. People cordon off parts of their lives that may be unpleasant. This way, they can go on living as if the unpleasantness isn't there. President Bill Clinton learned to compartmentalize from his mother, Virginia Clinton Kelley, as a coping mechanism. She wrote in her autobiography, *Leading with My Heart: My Life*, "Whatever is in someone's past is past, and I don't need to know about it…When bad things do happen, I brainwash myself to put them out of my mind."[13] Brainwashing oneself, says Os Guinness, is another term for suppressing truth. "Convenient in the short run, it is disastrous in the long run," he says. "It should be named clearly as the lack of integrity that it is."[14]

7. You see it as your duty to lie

Families often keep dark secrets hidden by skirting the truth. Executives may cover up the truth by calling whistleblowers critical and self-righteous. Presumably, since spies lie for a living (pretending to be someone or something they are not), they feel it's their duty to lie.

Valerie Plame was a former CIA agent who worked undercover for two decades. In 2003 her cover was blown and her shadowy career ended when her name was leaked to a newspaper columnist. She and her husband claim the exposure came in retribution for the fact that he claimed the White House had exaggerated intelligence to justify the invasion of Iraq. What did she learn from all her years as a spy? She said, "Most people are more than willing to talk about themselves."[15]

WHY PEOPLE LIE

National Geographic ran a cover story on the subject, "Why People Lie."[16] In the article, the author used a pie chart to show the reasons why people lie. According to the research cited, 36 percent of lies are "to protect yourself." Of this number, 22 percent of people tells lies of "personal transgression." In other words, they are attempting to cover up a misdeed or a mistake. Another 14 percent are lies of "avoidance," in an attempt to escape or evade other people.

On the other hand, 44 percent of lies are "to promote yourself." Of these, 16 percent lie for "economic advantage." They are hoping to gain financial benefits. Around 15 percent lie for "personal advantage," that is, looking for some benefit beyond money.

Another 8 percent are for "self-impression," that is, to shape a positive image of ourselves, whereas 5 percent of lies are for "humor." We like to make people laugh.

Some 11 percent of lies are "to impact others." These include 5 percent of lies that are ostensibly "altruistic," or to help others. Another 4 percent are actually "malicious," in which the intent is to hurt others. What we might call "social" or "polite lies" make up 2 percent. These are told to uphold social rules or to avoid rudeness.

Finally, the motive of 9 percent of lies is "unclear." While 2 percent may be classified as "pathological," in which the liar ignores or disregards reality, the motive for the other 7 percent is unknown. The motive is unclear, even to ourselves.

In studying the motivation for lying, psychologist Bruno Verschuere says, "The truth comes naturally, but lying takes effort and a sharp, flexible mind."[17] He says children learn to lie between the ages of two and five and lie the most when they are testing their independence.

WHY PEOPLE RESPECT A TRUTH TELLER

Some people always tell the truth, even if it hurts. And they don't seem to feel any obligation to couch their words in softer language or make any attempt to be tactful. If the dress makes you look fat, they will just come right out and say it. After all, you want the truth, right?

Others tell the truth, but they are conscious of other people's feelings, so they look for a way to speak the truth without slashing, smashing, piercing, or cutting. They try to remain truthful but tactful. They employ language that helps soften the blow. Most of us want to know the truth; but we seldom like to be knocked off our feet with it.

The question becomes, then, how to find the balance. How can we be more like Jesus, who was "full of grace and truth" (John 1:14)? He spoke the truth and he was also gracious. Those are qualities worth emulating.

The honest thing to do

In the years before he became president of the United States, Theodore Roosevelt was a cowboy in Montana and Wyoming. He worked like all the people he employed, sometimes longer than the others because he would go to his room and write after the day's work was done.

One day he found one of his ablest cowboys about to brand an unbranded stray. Roosevelt dismissed him on the spot. The cowboy could not understand why Roosevelt would be so hard-nosed about it. Theodore explained, "A man who will steal *for* me will steal *from* me. You're fired."[18]

Obviously, he believed there was no substitute for honesty.

Reggie Damone was a forty-seven-year-old McDonald's employee. While walking in December 2007, he picked up an envelope containing a check for $185,000. Damone received and depended on food stamps, but he resisted the temptation to cash the check. Instead he took a bus to the bank and returned the check so they could see that the woman who had written it got it back. For his honesty, the woman rewarded Damone with a $50 bill.[19]

His honesty spoke volumes about his integrity.

In the 1980s, the manufacturers of Tylenol learned someone had tampered with their capsules by lacing them with poison. Instead of trying to cover up the truth or minimize the impact of what had happened, Johnson & Johnson went before television cameras and apologized to the American people. As Larry King observed, "Their public relations approach in essence was not to use a public relations approach. They told the truth."[20]

The result was that the public retained confidence in their product and the company has become respected for its forthright approach.

The confident thing to do

A person who tells the truth can be confident because he knows his words have a firm foundation. Thomas Jefferson recognized this. He said, "Nothing gives one person so much advantage over another as to remain cool and unruffled under all circumstances."[21] It's hard to remain unruffled if you're skirting the truth.

Zig Ziglar said, "You can't consistently perform in a manner that is inconsistent with the way you see yourself."[22] If you are uncertain of the truth and you build a case against yourself, it's like using a microscope. A microscope is excellent for magnifying small things, but it cannot work with great ones. To avoid building a case against yourself, advises John L. Mason, "multiply your prayer time, divide the truth from a lie, subtract negative influences, and add God's Word."[23]

In 1957 the Russians launched Sputnik, a satellite that orbited the earth and came back in an hour and a half. A month later, they launched *Sputnik 2*, and this time a dog was on board. Americans were unhappy that the Russians had entered space first. Then when Russian cosmonaut Yuri Gagarin became the first man to orbit the earth, many Americans were livid. Where was our space program? It was embarrassing that we couldn't get anything off the ground, literally and figuratively.

To save face and to quiet all the talk about the Russians being first, the National Aeronautics and Space Administration (NASA) introduced the Mercury Seven, the first seven men chosen to be American astronauts. They offered sincere congratulations to the Russians, but they were clearly disappointed that the American program was behind.

However, a gut-level honest approach saved the day. John Glenn, one of the Mercury Seven, "had a secret. Be blunt. Be truthful." He told reporters, "They just beat the pants off us. There's no kidding ourselves about that. But now that the space age has begun, there's going to be plenty of work for everybody."[24]

Not everybody liked what he said, but it was the truth. Because

Glenn was honest, he could speak with confidence. Being truthful is the confident thing to do.

The courageous thing to do

People who tell the truth and act with integrity show great courage in the process. If you have ever seen the motion picture *Chariots of Fire*, then you know the story of Scottish runner Eric Liddell, who prepared to run the 100 meters in the 1924 Olympics. He almost certainly would have won a gold medal, but when he learned the heats took place on a Sunday, his religious convictions would not permit him to run.

Instead, he began training for the 400 meters, which was not his strongest event, and no one expected him to win a gold medal in that race. But he did, much to his country's delight. Then to the surprise of many, he made the decision to become a missionary to China. He could have brought honor to his country and fame, fortune, and glory for himself had he pursued a career as an athlete.

In the lead-up to World War II, Liddell put his life in danger more than once as he brought supplies to the school where he taught in China. On one occasion, armed thieves attacked and robbed him. On another he was shot at.

He was put in a Japanese internment camp after the war started. Even there he worked tirelessly, teaching as well as organizing cricket, softball, and tennis games for the children. When he noticed one teenager's shoes were worn out, Eric gave him his extra pair, the very shoes he had worn in the Olympic Games.

After years in the camp, he began suffering terrible headaches. Camp doctors believed he had a brain tumor. One evening in 1945, he slipped into a coma and died at the age of forty-three. Much later, China revealed that he had been included in a prisoner exchange, but rather than going free, he gave up his place to a pregnant woman.[25]

Liddell was a man of courage, and it showed up in so many ways, both in how he lived and in how he spoke. It wasn't easy to speak up when his convictions led him in a direction opposite of what most people expected him to do. It wasn't easy to speak up and trade places with the pregnant woman. If he had kept quiet, he might have been free to seek a better quality of medical care than what he received in the intern-ment camp. But he lived and spoke as a man of courage and integrity.

The gracious thing to do

Stuart Briscoe wrote that shortly before he married his fiancée, Jill, his father-in-law said to him, "Stuart, if you drive over to Austria and go to the little border town of Feldkirk, at a certain address you will find a person who has some funds which I have placed in your name. Go and collect them and you will have more than enough for three weeks' vacation on the continent of Europe."

Stuart did as recommended, met the person, and claimed what his father-in-law had promised. He found that the funds had indeed been placed to his account.[26]

Had he traveled around Europe bragging about his newfound wealth and pretending it was the product of his own work, it would have been insulting to his father-in-law and far removed from the truth. The fact is that he graciously boasted about the generosity of his father-in-law instead of falsely boasting about his own achievements.

Telling the truth is frequently the most gracious thing to do. Integrity demands that we be honest about how much we owe to others. The world does occasionally seem to produce a self-made man, but even then, if the truth were known, someone likely gave him a break some-where along the way. Or someone saw potential in a gifted woman and introduced her to the right people at the right time.

A friend who has had some admirable accomplishments in his long career told me one story after another about others who had helped him. One man gave him helpful books early in his life because he saw that the young man had potential. Another man suggested he submit a resumé to an enterprise that provided him with a job that gave him valuable experience. Still another man called him with an offer that opened the door to a new venture that paved the way for even further achievement.

Instead of boasting about his accomplishments, my friend speaks humbly and convincingly about the contributions others have made throughout his years of service. People respect a truth teller because being honest is the gracious way to live.

The kind thing to do

Peggy Noonan, a weekly columnist for the *Wall Street Journal*, has collected a lot of stories about Ronald Reagan, for whom she used to write speeches. She says she never heard a critical anecdote except once. She met a man who had once worked in a hotel restaurant in the desert of the Southwest, and one night Reagan came in and said he had a reservation. He was alone. For some reason, his name wasn't in the book. But Reagan was well-known, and they kindly asked him to wait a few minutes. However, Reagan lost his temper, berated the man, and left.

Noonan was delighted to hear this story because it seemed so out of character. The man who told her the story agreed but assured her it really happened. She asked if he had ever seen Reagan again. The man said, "Oh sure, the next morning when he came to apologize."[27]

Everybody makes mistakes, but to be kind enough to return and apologize is commendable. Noonan adds that Reagan's detractors will sometimes declare he was lazy or naïve or a bore. "But," she declares, "they never say he was low or unkind or dishonest or untrustworthy." People respect a truth teller because being honest is the kind thing to do.

Leo Buscaglia said, "Too often we underestimate the power of a touch, a smile, a kind word, a listening ear, an honest compliment, or the smallest act of caring, all of which have the potential to turn a life around."[28]

The thing you do in good conscience

If you were to take the word *conscience* apart and look for its origins, you would find it consists of two words: *with* and *knowledge*. So conscience has to do with the knowledge you possess. But it goes a bit beyond just possessing knowledge, because our consciences tend to hold us accountable for the knowledge we have.

In other words, if we know something is not good for us, either morally or financially or even physically, and we do it anyway, our conscience may prick us on the inside to alert us we have crossed the line. We have acted in a way that conflicts with what we know.

Some Native Americans believe the conscience is like a cube that spins inside the heart. When we do something we know we shouldn't, it begins to spin. The cube's edges and corners are sharp, so when we first violate our conscience, the cube cuts us and we feel pain. But the more we do that same thing, the more the edges and corners of the cube become worn. After a while, it may spin as always, but it doesn't have the same effect.

However, when we pay attention to our conscience, and we don't allow it to become insensitive, it helps us to live with integrity. When we live with integrity, our conscience is clear. As John Wooden, the great UCLA basketball coach, said, "There is no pillow as soft as a clear conscience."[29]

Ken Blanchard contends that ethical behavior is good for business. He believes some people are not convinced of that and consequently make ethical behavior a low priority. However, when he and Norman Vincent Peale worked on the book *The Power of Ethical Management*, they discovered that companies that are successful over the long term tend to be ethical companies.

On the other hand, companies that take advantage of their customers, their suppliers, or their employees may show a higher profit margin short-term. But the trust they lose may become permanent. He even suggested that employees who feel the company treats them unfairly may try to get even by stealing supplies, padding expense accounts, calling in sick when they are well, and engaging in other dishonest behavior.

Blanchard declares that astute business managers know that ethical practices go hand in hand with business success. Kenneth T. Derr, one-time chairman of the Chevron Corporation, said, "There's no doubt in my mind that being ethical pays, because I know that, in our company, people who sleep well at night work better during the day."[30]

Honesty really is the best policy. Be a truth teller. You can live with yourself and sleep at night with a clear conscience.

Chapter Seven

THE POWER OF SILENCE

- -

An ancient proverb holds that even a fool is thought to be
wise if he keeps silent. In this chapter, you will learn to identify
occasions when saying nothing is the wisest form of speech.

- -

*"Silence fertilizes the deep place where
personality grows. A life with a peaceful
center can weather all storms."*

NORMAN VINCENT PEALE[1]

The ability to speak is a gift. We take it for granted, of course, because it's something we learn at a young age and keep doing until we die. Occasionally, something interferes with our ability to speak. We are "at a loss for words." Or we are choked with emotion and cannot speak. Or sometimes a physical condition affects the voice box and causes a person to lose his or her voice.

A friend told me about an acquaintance who underwent surgery on the carotid artery. In the process the surgeon had to move the vagus nerve aside. It apparently did not like this stimulation, and when the patient awoke from surgery, he could only speak in a whisper. The situation, said my friend, may resolve itself over time, but the surgeon made no promises. He comforted the patient with the fact that he did not suffer a stroke.

The ability to speak is precious to us. Even though we take it for granted, we cherish the ability to speak. We even talk about the right to free speech being part of the first amendment to the United States Constitution. Specifically, it says, "Congress shall make no law respecting an establishment of religion, or prohibiting the free exercise thereof; or abridging the freedom of speech, or of the press; or the right of the people peaceably to assemble, and to petition the Government for a redress of grievances."

So, with free speech being one of our guaranteed rights and such a cherished blessing, why a chapter on silence? Because silence is golden.

SILENCE IS GOLDEN

At least that's what Thomas Carlyle, the English poet, said. But that thought was not original with him. He translated it from the Swiss inscription: "Sprecfien ist silbern, Schweigen ist golden" (Speech is silver, silence is golden).[2]

Epictetus, the Greek Stoic philosopher, is credited with saying, "We have two ears and one mouth so that we can listen twice as much as we speak."[3] Does it disconcert you, as it does many people, when participants on television talk shows speak over one another until we cannot understand either party? It seems many of us have a difficult time keeping silent while waiting for the other person to finish his or her thought.

Maybe it has something to do with our attention span. Microsoft has conducted research showing people on average lose focus after only eight seconds. Gary D. Foster says, "This means people now have shorter attention spans than goldfish."[4] He thinks this phenomenon matches our desire for instant everything. With shorter attention spans also comes shorter patience. We want what we want when we want it.

But engaging in intentional silence is also worth considering. At one extreme end of the talk-silence continuum are those who take a vow of silence. Monastic silence is a practice of various religious traditions, but it is often associated with Roman Catholic monks. Theophilus, patriarch of Alexandria, said the virtue of silence was on a par with faith itself. In a letter around AD 400, he wrote, "Monks—if they wish to be what they are called—will love silence and the Catholic faith, for nothing at all is more important than these two things."[5]

Perhaps you heard of the monk who entered a monastery and took a vow of silence. This monastery was unique, however, in that it permitted its monks to say two words every five years. The living conditions were spartan, the monks had to work hard at various kinds of physical labor, they were expected to spend considerable time in prayer, and the food rations were meager. So at the end of the first five years, when given the opportunity to speak his two words, the monk said, "Bed hard."

Another five years passed, marked by the same conditions. When given his second opportunity to speak, the monk said, "Food bad."

After another five years of hard work, much prayer, and miserable conditions, his supervisor gave him his third opportunity to speak. The monk said, "I quit!"

His supervisor said, "I'm not surprised. You've done nothing but complain for the past fifteen years!"

Silence is difficult for most of us. And when we do get the opportunity to speak, we don't always say the right things. So, whether silence comes easily to us or not, most of us recognize there are times when it is better to say nothing.

Yet, we talk...and talk.

WHY DO WE TALK SO MUCH?

Some have a bigger problem than others with talking too much. In an earlier chapter, I mentioned a man who told a woman who lived in the same apartment building that she talked too much. Many of us may have been tempted to say the same thing, but we were uncomfortable with being that direct. For some people, words flow in a garrulous fashion that resembles water flowing from a hydrant. So why do we talk so much?

To fill the silence

Many people are uncomfortable with silence. In radio and television, "dead air" is one of the worst things that can occur. Technicians, producers, and directors nearly panic when any unintended period of silence happens and no sound is being transmitted. Consequently, since we have been raised in an era when media try to fill every second with some kind of noise, silence can be deafening! So we fill the space with our noise, primarily talking.

However, when we jump into a conversation to fill the "dead air," we may be doing someone else an injustice. "Pauses are sometimes another person's thinking time; they are also moments for imparting gravity or emphasis onto what has already been said. Some people like to take a moment to think and compose their answer carefully."[6]

Our discomfort with silence may push us to interrupt or to judge prematurely that a person is finished with his or her conversation. We may even cause them to lose their train of thought if we jump in too quickly.

To entertain

Halle Tecco, a blogger on *Huffington Post,* did some research in which she asked a talkative friend, Erica, what she thought about Freud's theory of oral fixation. This is the notion that when children fail to resolve conflicts during the first eighteen months of life, they tend to develop maladaptive oral fixations later in life—such as overeating, smoking, chewing on toothpicks or straws, nail biting, and overtalking.

Erica responded, "I think I talk to fill the silence. If everyone is quiet, it makes me feel like people aren't enjoying themselves…and I'm all about making sure everyone feels welcome and is having a good time."[7]

If we interpret silence as boredom, we may want to fill it with talking, because the eleventh commandment for many people seems to be, "Thou shalt not be boring."

The sound of our own voice

Some people just love to hear the sound of their own voice, and that appears to be most of us. Science has shown that our favorite topic of conversation is ourselves. We spend 60 percent of our conversation time talking about ourselves, and that rises to 80 percent when we're chatting on social media.[8]

A friend (we'll call him Ray) admitted to an embarrassing situation when he was taking a graduate course at the university in his town.

During a class discussion phase, he answered the professor's question and just kept on talking, unaware of how much he was dominating the discussion. Finally, when he paused for a breath, the professor said, "Thank you, Ray. I think we're all aware of your excellent verbal skills. Now let's see if anyone else in the class would like to speak."

Ray wanted to crawl under a table. The professor had hit the nail on the head and his gentle rebuke was a helpful correction. Ray later heard of an acronym that has helped him, based on the word WAIT. It means, "Why Am I Talking?" If we become aware that we are talking too much and dominating the conversation, it is helpful to say to ourselves silently, "WAIT! Why am I talking?" Then respond to our own rebuke by falling silent so others can speak.

We like our stories better

Fred went to a class reunion. The person in charge encouraged people to stand and relate amusing incidents that happened to them when they were in school. Fred said he listened to several stories and was amazed at how short his attention span was. In no time, he was wishing this would end and they would move on to something else. He says he had a flash of insight as he sat there, listening to the stories drone on: "My stories are more interesting than anyone else's—but only to me."

That's how everyone feels. We like our own stories best. And because we like them best, we prefer to talk rather than listen. As we tell our stories, we get to relive the incident. Especially if it was pleasant, we experience joy all over again. But even if it's a sad story, maybe we get a special satisfaction from eliciting sympathy from a new group of people.

CONTROLLING THE URGE TO TALK

Stereotypes abound when it comes to talking. Women talk more than men, right? Tecco says her research shows women use about twenty thousand words a day, which is about thirteen thousand more than the average man. She admits there's still a lot of research and debate about those figures.[9]

Another stereotype says Italians talk with their hands. That may be true, but I have observed that many people talk with their hands.

Another stereotype says people in the northern United States talk faster than people from the South. Marissa Fessenden says research has shown this is true. States known for producing fast talkers are Oregon, Minnesota, Massachusetts, Kansas, and Iowa. She says the five slowest are North Carolina, Alabama, South Carolina, Louisiana, and Mississippi. The difference, however, isn't huge. Fast talkers manage to utter six words to every five words spoken by a slow talker.[10]

Even if we may be predisposed to be talkative, we don't have to give in to those urges. We can control our urge to talk. But how?

Don't feel obligated to say something

If you don't have an opinion, don't feel obligated to give one. Someone said, "Blessed is the man who, having nothing to say, cannot be persuaded to say it."

Henry David Thoreau observed workmen stringing wires through a meadow close to Walden. He went to investigate, and the workmen explained this was the new invention, the telegraph. One of them said, "Haven't you heard? With the telegraph, the people in Maine can communicate with the people in Florida."

Thoreau whimsically responded, "But what if the people in Maine have nothing to say to the people in Florida?"[11]

Rather shocking to contemplate, isn't it—actually having nothing to say? With a 24/7 news cycle, there's always something to say, right? Not necessarily. And if you have nothing to say, don't feel obligated to say it.

Use the traffic light strategy

Mark Goulston tells about an embarrassing incident that happened to him after his book, *Just Listen*, was published. He was talking to his friend Marty Nemko, host of a radio show in San Francisco. Mark didn't realize he was talking too much and that he had begun to annoy Marty, until Marty said, "Mark, for an expert on listening, you need to talk less and listen more."

Ouch! Then Marty gave him a strategy that may be helpful to many people. It's called the Traffic Light Rule. The rule says that in the first twenty seconds of conversation with someone, the light is green. The person likes you and enjoys the conversation, as long as you remain relevant. In the next twenty seconds, the light turns yellow. Now the other person is losing interest and is beginning to think you are a bit too chatty or perhaps even long-winded. At the forty-second mark, your light turns red. You may, on occasion, want to run that red light. But typically, you'd better stop or you will be in danger.[12]

Pay attention to others' body language

People are often good at giving us clues that our time is up and it's time to let someone else talk. Ever get the eye roll when you start to talk? How about the tapping foot? Maybe they are staring at you as if they're interested, but that tapping foot is sending a different signal. Or maybe, as you began to elaborate on your subject, their eyes begin to glaze over and they look distracted. If people throw out irrelevant yeahs and uh-huhs but do not encourage you to elaborate, you are probably talking too much.[13]

If you are seeing these signs, it's a pretty good indication you are overtalking. And being aware is the first step in correcting the problem.

THE ADVANTAGES OF SILENCE

If silence is a virtue that we ought to pursue, what are the advantages we can expect to receive by intentionally practicing it?

Opportunity for growth

When noise constantly floods our lives, we seldom have the opportunity to stop and examine ourselves. Although too much introspection is unhealthy, occasionally looking at ourselves with discernment can be highly profitable. What are your strengths and weaknesses? Are you building on your strengths? Are you minimizing the effects of your weaknesses?

We all want things to get better for our businesses, for our families, and for us personally. Jim Rohn, the business philosopher, said, "For things to get better, you have to get better. For things to change, you have to change." He also said, "The most important question to ask on the job is not 'What am I getting?' The most important question to ask is, 'What am I becoming?'"[14]

Getting into a quiet place, where we put other concerns aside and concentrate on who and what we are becoming, is an issue of paramount importance.

Bobb Biehl suggests three ways we can grow in our work. We can grow up by earning promotions and growing into them. We can grow sideways by relating to and getting to know our friends and peers better, learning how to relate better socially. And we "can grow down by going deeper into a subject, or deeper into your character."[15]

I don't know any way to do that apart from the discipline of silence, the discipline of examining who we are and where we are in our growth. Edwin Markham put it this way:

> We are blind until we see
> That in the human plan
> Nothing is worth the making
> If it does not make the man.
> Why build these cities glorious
> If the man unbuilded goes?
> In vain we build the world
> Unless the builder also grows.[16]

Getting into a quiet place, where silence can give us the time and space to focus on our own growth, is an important step in tremendous personal development.

To be more effective

We all want to be more effective. But if we never slow down long enough to quiet our minds, quiet our spirits, and spend some time in reflection, our effectiveness will likely plateau. We'll do what we do, but not grow and advance as we should.

Harvey Mackay suggests that a company's best people may spend their most productive time staring at the wall. He tells a story about a manager who couldn't use his tickets for Schubert's *Unfinished*

Symphony, so he gave them to his efficiency expert and received the following report after the performance.

1. The four oboe players had nothing to do for long periods of time. Some of them should be dismissed and their work spread over the whole orchestra.

2. Forty violins played the same note. This section should be cut to avoid unnecessary duplication. The same effect could be achieved using an electronic amplifier.

3. There is no point in all the effort absorbed in the playing of semiquavers. All notes should be rounded to the nearest quaver. This way trainees and lower-grade operators could be used at considerable savings.

4. There is no point in the horns repeating passages that have already been handled by the strings. If these duplications were removed, the concert could be reduced to twenty minutes. If Schubert had been more efficient, he might have been able to finish his symphony.

Obviously, we don't want to achieve efficiency at the cost of creativity. But as Mackay points out, "If you discover one of your executives looking at the wall, like the oboe player, instead of filling out a report, go over and congratulate him or her…They're thinking. It's the hardest, most valuable task any person performs."[17]

Thinking is best done in silence.

To learn

Learning requires some degree of silence. We never learn anything when we are talking. Obviously, we already know what we are talking about, but when we listen, we learn. When the other person has a chance to share their viewpoint, their knowledge, the benefit of their research, study, and life lessons, we have the opportunity to learn.

John Mason observed that "what we learn about another person will always result in a greater reward than what we tell him about ourselves."[18] As fascinating as we think our stories are and as scintillating as our experiences have been, we learn nothing unless we listen to the other person's stories and opinions.

The power of listening to teach you cannot be overestimated. Doug Firebaugh said his mentor taught him, "The last word in listen is 'ten'… Listening is ten times more powerful, and success-attracting in the long-run, than talking."[19] To learn we must listen, and to listen we must close our mouths and be silent. Only then will the learning take place.

To think more clearly

To tune in to better thinking, we must tune out the noise that so easily distracts us. The old German proverb says, "Silence is a fence around wisdom."[20] Wisdom seldom comes marching down the street, accompanied by a bass drum. Wisdom comes in quiet reflection on life.

When we quiet our minds and hearts and reflect on life, we can begin to think more clearly. We may even begin to hear what is not being said. Peter Bregman said, "Silence is a greatly underestimated source of power. In silence, we can hear not only what is being said, but also what is not being said. In silence, it can be easier to reach the truth."[21]

Recognizing the need to grow, learn, and develop, Oprah Winfrey declared, "You have to move up to another level of thinking, which is true for me and everybody else. Everybody has to learn to think differently, bigger, to be open to possibilities."[22] It's hard to imagine this happening apart from meditation and reflection in silence.

THE DISCIPLINE OF SILENCE

We have to discipline ourselves to be silent. Hardly anyone likes discipline. Yet we never accomplish great things without it. If you want a better physique, it takes discipline. It takes exercise, maybe some push-ups, definitely some push-back from the table. If you want a college degree, it takes discipline. If you want a better life, it takes discipline. A better you? Discipline.

So a part of your becoming better is learning when to speak and when to be silent.

A time to be silent

The wise man said there is "a time to be silent and a time to speak" (Ecclesiastes 3:7). No thinking person would suggest you should keep quiet when it's time to speak. Mitch Albom developed a friendship with a rabbi named Albert Lewis in Detroit. His nickname for the rabbi was Reb. He told Mitch a story about a man who buried his wife. At the gravesite, the man stood by the rabbi, with tears falling down his face.

"I loved her," he whispered.

The Reb nodded.

"I mean…I really loved her." The man broke down. "And…I almost told her once."

The Reb looked at Mitch sadly. "Nothing haunts like the things we don't say."[23]

Obviously, the man should have spoken up. He should have told his wife he loved her. How sad to think he missed all those opportunities.

Having said that, however, there is a time to keep silent. When we don't know what to say, it's better not to say anything. In times of extreme grief, when a wife has lost her husband or parents have lost their child, a hug says more than anything we can relate verbally. At times of profound emotions, silence speaks volumes.

Both Abraham Lincoln and Mark Twain are credited for saying, "Better to remain silent and be thought a fool than to speak out and remove all doubt."

Recognize when it's a time to keep silent.

Learning to shut down unproductive thinking

Sometimes even silence is not helpful if our thinking is unproductive. I read a story about two monks who were traveling from one town to another. They came to a great puddle of water and noticed a young woman standing there, unable to make up her mind whether to wade in and get wet or take a large detour around the puddle. One monk didn't hesitate. He approached her and offered to take her on his back across the puddle. Afterward, the woman got down, thanked the monk, and she and the monks went on their way.

A few hours later, the other monk asked the one who had carried the woman, "How could you do that? You know we're not supposed to do things like that. How could you carry a woman on your back?"

The helpful monk said, "I put her down right after we crossed the puddle. It seems you have been carrying her in your mind for hours."[24]

Obviously, silence is not helpful if we allow our minds to dwell on unproductive and negative things. This is where the discipline begins to help us, to intentionally set our minds on other things. People who have studied the thinking process tell us there are some natural laws that govern the way we think. Our minds operate on two levels—the conscious and the unconscious. The conscious mind deals with whatever is happening now. It deals with awareness and uses facts, logic, and reasoning. The subconscious mind is very complex. It records every thought and experience, every emotion, every sensory impression we experience all our lives. It files away that data and cross-references it. When we encounter any situation, it tends to sort through the stored data, compare this situation with other situations we have had, and chooses a response that we have found most satisfactory in similar situations in the past. It sends this information up to the conscious mind, and we almost always follow its suggestions.[25]

The conscious and the unconscious mind cooperate in this way in many hundreds, perhaps thousands of decisions every day, from getting up in the morning, to brushing our teeth, to driving the car. However, if we have fed a lot of negative information into our minds over the years, that's all it has to work with. Consequently, it can feed back to us only the negative garbage it has ingested. We are what we think.

So in silence, in meditation, in purposeful thinking, we shut off the negative. We throw out the trash. We begin to build a better life by talking about the good things, listening to the good things, and reading the good things.

Some negative ingredients slow us down. Some will cause us to limp through life. Other negative ingredients will kill us. They will kill our ambition, kill our desire, kill our strong feelings, kill our compassion. So we have to watch like a hawk what gets poured into our mental factory. As surely as we live, what gets poured in eventually comes out, and we want it to be positive.

No wonder James Allen said, "You are today where your thoughts have brought you. You will be tomorrow where your thoughts take you."[26]

Problem solving

One of the advantages of learning the discipline of silence is the ability to focus on problem solving. Every problem has a solution, but it often requires concentrated thinking, focusing our attention to discover the answer.

Before Norman Vincent Peale achieved fame with his book *The Power of Positive Thinking,* and before he was pastor of the acclaimed Marble Collegiate Church in New York City, he served a congregation in Syracuse, New York—the University Methodist Church. In his congregation was a man who was considered by some to be the greatest businessman Syracuse ever had. His name was Harlow B. Andrews. He was reportedly one of the early inventors of the dishwasher. He also had a reputation for having the most acute financial sense of anyone in that area.

Based on Andrews's reputation as a man of wisdom, Peale took his problems to him one day. Andrews listened as the young minister outlined his difficulties. When Peale had "run down a bit," Andrews asked him if that was all there was to his problem. When Peale nodded, Andrews waved his hands with a sweeping motion as though he were piling up a lot of stuff. He grinned and said, "Quite a pile. Sure is a big problem, isn't it?"

Then he said, "Come here, son, let's walk around this problem." Then Andrews made as though to poke at the pile. Peale noticed his big rough forefinger. Arthritis had caused that finger to be crooked, but, reported Peale, "he could point mighty straight with that crooked finger."

"Every problem," Andrews said, "has a soft spot. I've learned that fact over the years. Every problem has a soft spot. When you find it, the problem can be broken apart, and you can put a right solution together."

So he proceeded to walk around the problem, muttering to himself. Then he said, "Ah, we've got it. Here is that soft spot," meanwhile wiggling that forefinger into it. "Let's handle it at this point. This is the essence of your difficulties. Let's take it from here and go forward."

Being a religious man himself, Andrews advised the young minister to apply some positive faith, pray some big prayers, and believe he would get big results.[27]

As you think through your problems, whatever they are, as you silently meditate and wrestle with the details of your situation, remember that every problem has a solution. If you study it with focused attention, you will come to see where the "soft spot" is, where the problem might be vulnerable to attack. Start there and pursue your chosen course of action.

Silence. It's almost like a foreign language to many of us. Our minds and thoughts are inundated with noise all day long, whether it's streaming from the television, CDs, the car radio, or coworkers who engage us in conversation. Intentional silence is something you may have to struggle to achieve. But if you find a place to be alone to think, meditate, reflect, plan, and just be silent, it will make a positive difference in your life.

Part 3

ATTITUDE
BEFORE WORDS

Chapter Eight

YOUR ATTITUDE
SAYS EVERYTHING

Every renovation project involves three steps: planning,
demolition, and construction. Here you will learn to
reconstruct your attitude by (1) crafting your approach,
(2) renewing your mind, and (3) choosing your words.

---

*"Our speech is never truly accidental.
If you listen to someone talk for long enough,
you will know what kind of person he or she is...
A mouth opens, and out pops a heart."*

TIM STAFFORD[1]

Words do not live in a vacuum. They always come from an attitude, and attitude is the atmosphere in which words live and breathe. A positive attitude produces positive words. A negative attitude produces negative words. Your attitude says everything.

Vanderlei de Lima is a small man. He stands five feet five and weighs less than 120 pounds. But the Brazilian has a big heart. At the 2004 Olympics in Athens, he ran the marathon and won the bronze medal for third place. He should have been first.

De Lima was leading the race with about three miles to go when a deranged protestor from Ireland burst out of the crowd and hurled himself into the runner. The impact forced him off the course and into the crowd. As you can imagine, de Lima was stunned and shaken, but he gathered himself and resumed the race. Unfortunately, he could not make up the lost seconds and he could not regain first place.

Nevertheless, when he entered the stadium, he punched the air with his fists and ran with arms outstretched, almost as if he were a human airplane. Full of joy, as he received the olive wreath crown, he said, "It is a festive moment. It is a unique moment. Most athletes never have this moment."

True, but most athletes don't get knocked off the course either. Yet he never complained. He said, "The Olympic spirit prevailed again… I was able to medal for myself and my country."[2]

What enabled him to rejoice when he could have been bitter? His terrific attitude.

Max Lucado suggests we could all take lessons from the attitudes of dogs and cats. The diary of a dog, for instance, might read like this:

8:00 a.m. Oh boy, dog food—my favorite.
9:30 a.m. Oh boy, a car ride—my favorite.
9:40 a.m. Oh boy, a walk—my favorite.
10:30 a.m. Oh boy, another car ride—my favorite.
11:30 a.m. Oh boy, more dog food—my favorite.
12:00 p.m. Oh boy, the kids—my favorite.
1:00 p.m. Oh boy, the yard—my favorite.
4:00 p.m. Oh boy, the kids again—my favorite.
5:00 p.m. Oh boy, dog food again—my favorite.
5:30 p.m. Oh boy, Mom—my favorite.
6:00 p.m. Oh boy, playing ball—my favorite.
8:30 p.m. Oh boy, sleeping in my master's bed—my favorite.

On the other hand, the diary of a cat may read something like this:

"Day 283 of my captivity. My captors continue to taunt me with bizarre little dangling objects. They dine lavishly on fresh meat while I'm forced to eat dry cereal. I'm sustained by the hope of escape and the mild satisfaction I derive from ruining a few pieces of furniture."

The cat goes on to describe how he was tempted to kill his captors by weaving through their walking feet. He decapitated a mouse and deposited the body on the kitchen floor. He's convinced the bird is an informant because the feathered creature speaks with the humans regularly. He suspects the bird of reporting on his every move.

There's more in that vein, but you can see the gist of each one. One is content while the other is conniving. One is grateful while the other gripes.

Then Lucado asks, "Which diary reads more like yours? Were your private thoughts made public, how often would the phrase 'Oh boy, my favorite' appear?"[3]

What's the difference? Attitude, of course.

Let's say, for the purposes of this chapter, that your attitude is less than positive. Most people, to be honest, could use some work on their attitude. So let's work on it.

CRAFTING YOUR APPROACH

How will you deal with your attitude, assuming you want it to improve? One of the first steps is to realize the truth about attitudes.

The truth about attitudes

Attitudes are habits of thought. Yogi Berra, whose quirky comments seem to include both humor and at least some truth, said, "Life is like baseball: it's 95 percent mental and the other half is physical."[4] Despite his unusual mathematical proportions, Berra understands that many of us underestimate how much the mind is involved in whether we succeed or fail. I say that to emphasize that habits are not limited to actions. Habits may also include attitudes.

Tom Haggai said, "I am convinced the steepest and most neglected slope of the learning curve is attitude, not aptitude."[5]

In a similar vein, Denis Waitley pointed out: "The winner's edge is not in a gifted birth, a high IQ, or in talent. The winner's edge is all in the attitude not aptitude. Attitude is the criterion for success."[6] Waitley added, "But you can't buy an attitude for a million dollars. Attitudes are not for sale."[7]

Many people underestimate the power of their attitude. They may not realize their attitude is affecting their performance far more than they can imagine. W. Clement Stone said, "There is a little difference in people but that little difference makes a big difference. The little difference is attitude. The big difference is whether it is positive or negative."[8]

Habits of attitude are formed the same way as habits of action. If we discover that a certain thought pattern gives us some type of pleasure or satisfaction, we are likely to repeat it and it becomes a habit. You might reason, How do people get satisfaction out of negative attitudes? What possible pleasure can there be in saying "I can't" to every challenge of life?

There is a fine line between action habits and thought habits. Before a habit of action is formed, we may try several ways of acting. We may practice a number of things before we choose the best one. But thoughts are rather nebulous. They can trigger emotional responses without any testing. The same thought can give us pleasure or pain, depending on the association we choose to give it. For instance, the thought of a red sports car might cause you thoughts of great pleasure. However, if you had an accident in a red sports car and suffered broken bones that took weeks to heal, involving much pain, discomfort, and loss of job benefits, it might change your attitude toward red sports cars.

In some countries snails are considered by many people to be delicacies. You will find them listed on the menus of expensive restaurants as "escargot." But even in those countries, some people like them and some do not, because they have tasted them. In the United States, very few people have ever tried eating snails, but chances are that most people have very definite attitudes toward the practice of eating snails. Most people have arbitrarily chosen to give this thought a negative association. This attitude gives more satisfaction, even though it is negative, than the satisfaction they imagine to be associated with the alternative. They simply cannot visualize any pleasure in eating a snail.

George Sweeting tells about a duck hunter and his outstanding dog. The dog had the ability, when his master shot a duck, to run out on top of the water to retrieve the duck. Yet the owner's hunting buddy didn't seem to notice the dog's unusual ability.

The hunter asked, "Did you notice anything unusual about my hunting dog?"

His buddy answered, "Yes, he can't swim!"

That's a silly example, of course, but do you ever wonder if some people are so hopelessly mired in a negative pattern of thinking that they can't see something positive when it stares them in the face?

The fact is that we all have the potential to learn to think that way unless we intentionally determine that we will change. It's up to us.

Everyone is responsible for their own attitudes. William James, the psychologist-philosopher, said, "The greatest discovery of my generation is that people can alter their lives by altering their attitudes of mind."[9]

When you are born, everybody makes your decisions for you. Someone else caters to your needs. But as you grow, you begin making decisions. Sometimes these conflict with what your parents would like for you to do. But you grow in your ability to make decisions so that by the time you are twenty, you are making just about all your own decisions.

The story is told about Abraham Lincoln, who was being advised to consider a certain person for a cabinet position. Lincoln was not pleased with the suggestion. He said, "I don't like the man's face."

The advisor responded, "Sir, he can't be held responsible for his face!"

But Lincoln differed. "Every man over forty is responsible for his face."[10]

We are also responsible for our attitudes. Once we understand this, we can begin to plan how we can change them.

Watch your attitude

A friend told me he was surprised one day when a big bird flew up from the side of the road. Its movements took him by such a surprise that he didn't get a good look at it, except that it was large.

What was that? he thought. *A hawk? An eagle?*

He noticed it had flown to a nearby tree and there was no other traffic, so my friend slowed down to get a better look. It was a vulture. Big, alert, and ugly. It had been feeding on some kind of carrion, road-kill, rotting meat. Vultures have the uncanny ability to find it because that's what they are looking for.

On the other hand, a hummingbird looks only for the tiny blossoms that contain sweet nectar. There are types of hummingbirds that can find these flowers, even in the desert. You may not see the blossoms because they may be partially hidden from view by the rocks. But the hummingbird finds it. Indeed, each bird finds exactly what it is looking for. And so will you. Your attitude will dictate what you find.

Your attitude about yourself. Someone observed that when it comes to believing in themselves, some people are agnostics.

Three men were working together. One said, "My best girl left me, I have a boring job, and my feet hurt."

The second man said, "I'm engaged to a beauty, I love this job, and I could dance all night."

The first man turned to the third guy and said, "He sure takes the fun out of wallowing in your own misery."

If you are in the habit of putting yourself down, minimizing your own skills, and doubting your abilities, you will limit yourself artificially. In fact, our greatest limitations are those we impose on ourselves. Before Roger Bannister first ran the mile in less than four minutes, that feat was considered humanly impossible. It had become a mythical barrier. Now that the world knows it can be done, multiplied hundreds of other athletes have achieved that goal. As of this writing, the world record is held by a Moroccan, who ran the mile in 3:43.13.

In the 1968 Olympics in Mexico City, American athlete Bob Beamon shocked the world with a long jump of more than 29 feet, a good two feet farther than any other man had ever before recorded. It was unbelievable! Before the event, if you had asked the world's authorities—the Olympic coaches—they would have said, "It can't be done." Yet it was done, and the current record is held by American Mike Powell at 29 feet, 4¼ inches.

Accomplishing these seemingly impossible feats is similar to overcoming faulty attitudes. It may seem impossible. But the place to begin is to develop a better attitude about yourself.

Your attitude about your circumstances. We all face tough circumstances from time to time. That's why we have to maintain a positive attitude in spite of those things.

A Little Leaguer was standing by the fence when a stranger approached him and asked, "Son, what's the score?"

"Fourteen to nothing," the boy replied, continuing to fix his gaze on the game.

The man was shocked. "You mean you're losing, fourteen to nothing?" The boy nodded. "Well, aren't you discouraged, young man?"

The boy replied, "Well, no, we haven't even been up to bat yet."[11]

Things may look bad, but you have to put them in perspective.

Speaking of baseball, Pat Williams tells a story about Hall of Fame player Stan Musial. One day a St. Louis Cardinals teammate came into the clubhouse whistling. He turned to Stan and said, "I feel great. My home life is happy. I'm in a groove. I feel like I'm going to get two hits today. Ever feel like that, Stan?"

Musial smiled at him and said, "Every day!"[12]

You may not currently feel like that every day, but you can develop an attitude that faces each day positively and expectantly.

Raymond Bottom told about his postman, John, who retired after thirty years of carrying the mail. Raymond said he missed John's friendly cheerfulness and little bits of neighborhood news. It seems John was afflicted with painful arthritis, but he never let it show or color his outlook on life. Each day when Raymond would ask, "How are you today?" John would smile broadly and reply, "Just right."

One day, Raymond persisted a little and asked, "Isn't your arthritis bothering you these days, John?"

John admitted it was bothering him some.

Raymond asked, "Then how can you say you feel just right?"

John said, "On my route I have a lady who is blind. There's a young girl in a wheelchair, paralyzed from the waist down from an automobile accident. And there's a man who had his leg amputated last year. But you know, they're about the nicest, most positive people on my route. After I talk to them, I praise God I'm as healthy as I am. And I ask him to give me the faith and courage they have."[13]

What a great attitude in spite of difficult circumstances.

Hugh Downs, television personality from 1945 to 1999, once said, "A happy person is not a person in a certain set of circumstances, but rather a person with a certain set of attitudes."[14]

Your attitude about people. People can be delightful. They can also be terribly frustrating. The key to loving and accepting people is to have the right attitude. If we become cynical about people, it won't be long until we're cynical about ourselves. And that's an unfortunate attitude to take because it will hurt us in the long run.

Edwin Markham wrote a wonderful little poem, called "Outwitted," that captures the essence of what we have to do to improve our attitudes about people.

> He drew a circle that shut me out—
> Heretic, rebel, a thing to flout.
> But love and I had the wit to win:
> We drew a circle that took him in.[15]

Norman Vincent Peale reminds us that we have to be careful about allowing grudges and resentments to build up over time. "These things get lodged in the cracks and crevices of the mind," he warned. "Our failure in personal relationships may have to do largely with our own attitudes and with our own unwillingness to consider, modify and change those negative attitudes…Changed attitudes will change almost anything."[16]

I hope by now you're convinced that we have it within our power to change our attitudes. To do this, we must renew our minds.

RENEWING YOUR MIND

The apostle Paul used a powerful phrase when he wrote his letter to the Romans. He said, "Do not conform to the pattern of this world, but be transformed by the renewing of your mind" (Romans 12:2). The Greek word Paul used for "transformed" has the same root as our word *metamorphosis*. When we talk about a caterpillar becoming a butterfly, we use *metamorphosis* to explain the change.

So this is not referring to the kind of change we might observe in a man who wears jeans when working on his honey-do list around the house, but changes into a tuxedo to walk his daughter down the aisle on the day of her wedding. He doesn't look the same on the outside, but he is the same person on the inside.

What Paul urged us to consider is to undergo an internal change, a change of attitude, a renewing of the mind. The Greeks had an interesting way of handling the concept of "new." One Greek word, *neos*, means new in point of time. But the word *kainos* means new in point of character. A newly manufactured pencil is *neos*, but a person who has undergone a renewal of mind, character, and attitude is *kainos*. That's what Paul was getting at—we're not just turning over a new leaf, writing on a new page; rather we are approaching life with a more positive frame of mind. It's essentially a spiritual change.[17]

You may object that change is hard. It often is. But consider this: we all change.

We all change

Although change may be uncomfortable, we all do change in various ways. In the musical *The King and I*, the king of Siam is remembering how it used to be when everything was the same as it always had been. Now he laments his confusion over how things have changed. He says, "What was so was so. What was not was not. But now—is a puzzlement!"[18]

Do you ever feel puzzled about how to make needed changes in your life, especially anything as major as "the renewing of your mind"? You are not alone.

Change is a part of life. Astronaut James Irwin said, "You might think going to the moon was the most scientific project ever, but they literally 'threw us' in the direction of the moon. We had to adjust our course every ten minutes and landed only inside fifty feet of the five-hundred-mile radius of our target."[19] Life is full of changes.

It's true in the world of business. Mark J. Perry compiled a fascinating list of companies that were in the Fortune 500 in 1955 and were still there in 2016. Out of the 500, only 60 still exist on that list. In the group from 1955, several highly recognizable names are no longer on the list: American Motors, Studebaker, Zenith. Of the 60 still on the list, you will recognize these well-known companies: Boeing, Campbell Soup, General Motors, Kellogg. Then there are the newcomers who were not on the list in 1955: Facebook, eBay, Home Depot, Google, Microsoft, Netflix, Office Depot, and Target.[20]

It's all about change. Unfortunately, we all resist change.

We all resist change

In 1803, the British created a civil service position in which a man was required to stand on the cliffs of Dover with a spy glass. His job was to be on the lookout for invasion. He was to ring a bell if he saw the army of Napoleon Bonaparte approaching. Now that was all well and good for the time, but that job was not eliminated until 1945![21]

Sometimes there are good reasons why things are the way they have always been. You may never have had any reason to know that the standard railroad gauge (distance between rails) is four feet, eight and one half inches. This unusual number is that way because the people who built them were British expatriates and that's the way they were built in England.

Why did the British adopt that particular gauge? Because the people who built the pre-railroad tramways used that gauge. They in turn used that measurement because the people who built the tramways used the same standards and tools that their ancestors had used for building wagons.

But does anyone know why the wagons were built to that scale? Because any other size would not have fit the old wheel ruts in the roads. It turns out the first long-distance highways in Europe were built by Imperial Rome for the benefit of their legions. The ruts were first made by Roman war chariots. Four feet, eight and one half inches just happens to be the distance needed to accommodate the rear ends of two war horses.[22]

We all must change

Unless you think you are already perfect, you must change. To become all that we have the potential to become, we must alter our present habits and attitudes to bring them more in line with our goals, our dreams, and our best ambitions. Somebody observed, "Some people change jobs, mates, and friends, but never think of changing themselves."

Someone also observed, "The bend in the road is not the end of the road—unless you fail to make the turn." Turning requires change. Winston Churchill observed, "To improve is to change. To be perfect is to have changed often."[23]

The good news is that change is possible.

We all can change

Stephen Covey said, "Whatever your present situation, I assure you that you are not your habits. You can replace old patterns of self-defeating behavior with new patterns, new habits of effectiveness, happiness, and trust-based relationships."[24]

A human being is the only creature on earth that can remold and reshape himself or herself through insight. The only way to accomplish some kind of permanent change is through a change in attitude that comes from insight into oneself. Any other change, for any other reasons, will probably be temporary.

We must choose the right attitude toward change. Winston Churchill believed this. He said, "There is nothing wrong with change if it is in the right direction."[25]

On the other hand, a person who persistently resists change leads a dull, drab life. A person who accepts change finds joy in living because she is facing new experiences, new challenges, and new dimensions. Instead of resisting change, she faces it. She seeks to learn how to profit from change, how to improve, and how to better herself and those who depend on her. If she can develop a spirit of enthusiasm, she finds great rewards from setting goals and enjoying the thrill of the chase involved in most positive change.

Ty Boyd observed, "It is more than willingness to change that sets the true leaders apart. It is seeking out change and wringing every bit of potential out of it that takes you to the next horizon."[26]

We must take action to change. Dr. William Glasser said, "If you want to change attitudes, start with a change in behavior. In other words, begin to act the part, as well as you can, of the person you would rather be, the person you most want to become. Gradually, the old fearful person will fade away."[27]

Many people wait until they feel "inspired" to change. But what if inspiration never comes? Others wait until they "feel like it." But that is backwards. Often we have to act ourselves into changing.

Someone observed: "An act of your will, will lead you to action, and your positive action will lead to a positive attitude."[28]

CHOOSING YOUR WORDS

Life is all about choices. We choose every day in so many ways that we don't even realize how often we make choices. As I have pointed out earlier in this book, some choices are routine, like brushing our teeth or driving the car. Some choices we make because we have programmed ourselves over time to make those decisions in the same way every time.

In the next chapter we will talk about practical strategies for using positive words, but for now it's about the choices we make to do just that. These choices flow out of our attitudes. If we have improved our attitudes by renewing our minds, we will more likely make the better choices.

We are like Robert Frost, who wrote about choices:

> I shall be telling this with a sigh
> Somewhere ages and ages hence:
> Two roads diverged in a wood, and I—
> I took the one less traveled by,
> And that has made all the difference.[29]

Any day we choose to do so, we can make the choice to treat people differently, to speak to them differently, to look at them differently. We can do that today or tomorrow or next week or next month. The choice is ours.

Or we can choose to do nothing. We can tell ourselves that change is too difficult—I'm too far along in life to change now. Or I have my whole life before me—there will be plenty of time to change after I have tasted of whatever it is that I prefer to focus on right now.

Business philosopher Jim Rohn pointed out an uncomfortable truth: "We can pretend rather than perform. And if the idea of having to change ourselves makes us uncomfortable, we can remain as we are. We can choose rest over labor, entertainment over education, delusion over truth, and doubt over confidence. The choices are ours to make. But while we curse the effect, we continue to nourish the cause."[30]

So every day, we can choose the kinds of words we use. We need to choose carefully because they will have an impact on others.

- We can use words that are bitter or words that make people better.

- We can use words that communicate indifference or we can use words that inspire decisiveness.

- We can use words that spell lukewarmness or our words can engender enthusiasm.

- Our words can instill caution or we can inspire others to take calculated wholesome risks.

- Our words can communicate destructiveness or we can encourage development.

- Our words can reek of complaint or our words can be the fragrant language of encouragement.

- Our words can speak peace or we can stir up strife.

- We may come across as demanding or we can communicate invitation.

- We may speak words that spell progress or our words may stimulate regression.

- Our words may encourage solutions or they may cause the problem to be engrained more deeply.

- We may encourage people to be accountable or we may kindle irresponsibility.

Alfred Nobel was a Swiss chemist whose brother had passed away. When Alfred picked up the newspaper to read his brother's obituary, he discovered the newspaper had accidentally printed Alfred's obituary instead. The article described him as a man who had become rich by enabling people to kill each other in unprecedented numbers. It's true that he had invented dynamite and other powerful explosives. But seeing his life rendered in such negative tones shocked him and changed him. He determined to use his fortune to honor accomplishments that benefited humanity. He created the Nobel Peace Prize.[31]

Mr. Nobel chose to leave a positive influence rather than a negative one. You and I have the same choice to make. The way we treat people and the way we speak to them are choices. We can treat them with kindness or we can run roughshod over people. But know this: they will remember whether you "invented dynamite" or encouraged peace.

Stephen Covey often recounted the story of walking through the stacks of a library in Hawaii. By chance, he said, he pulled a book off the shelf and opened it to three sentences that literally changed his life. These are the sentences: "Between stimulus and response there is a space. In that space lies our freedom and power to choose our response. In our response lies our growth and our happiness."[32]

Those sentences that were so compelling to Covey are true of us as well. We too have the choice as to how we will respond to any stimulus in our lives. Our words, in turn, become a stimulus to other people— either to motivate them or to deflate them.

As Covey says, "This freedom-to-choose idea is both exhilarating and terrifying—exhilarating because it excites our sense of possibility, our sense of what we could do if we so choose, and terrifying because we're suddenly responsible—that is, 'response-able.' We are accountable."

So now we have the opportunity to be accountable, to make the right decision, to be determined to have attitudes that contribute positively instead of stirring up negativity. Theodore Roosevelt pointed out, "In any moment of decision, the best thing you can do is the right thing. The worst thing you can do is nothing."[33] Naturally, there is a whole range of options in between those two extremes.

You don't want to fall into the habit of being indecisive, living in the valley of indecision day after day. As Williams James said, "There is no more miserable human being than the one in whom nothing is habitual but indecision."[34]

Don't let that be said about you. Yours can be a legacy of good decisions, positive attitudes, and words that lift, inspire, and motivate. This is the person you can become by making the decision to change your attitude for the better.

Maybe you don't feel your attitude is all that bad. And maybe it isn't. But is there no room for improvement? With some sincere introspection, you can find ways to improve. You can discover new ways to communicate with others that elevates their opinion of themselves and improves their performance.

By taking responsibility for your own attitude toward yourself, your circumstances, and other people, by being willing to change, to renew your mind, and by making positive choices in the words you choose to use, this could be the beginning of a new day for you.

Chapter Nine

POSITIVE WORD POWER

A positive attitude is the basic building block of constructing positive words. In this chapter, you'll learn four practical strategies for how our attitude builds the foundation for positive words in us: (1) Practice self-affirmation, (2) compliment and praise others, (3) be tactful, and (4) use "power" words (I love you, I forgive you, I'm proud of you).

"By acting in a positive, pleasant, and optimistic way, you become a positive, optimistic, and enjoyable person."

BRIAN TRACY[1]

A positive attitude produces positive words. The place to begin using positive words—although it may seem uncomfortable at first—is on ourselves.

PRACTICE SELF-AFFIRMATION

It can be a fine line between self-affirmation and boasting. But an appropriate regard for oneself is commendable. Phillips Brooks said, "The true way to be humble is not to stoop until you are smaller than yourself but to stand at your real height against some higher nature that will show you what the real smallness of your greatest greatness is."[2] Next to the Creator of the universe, we are small indeed. But considering he made us in his image, that's pretty great!

You will undoubtedly face criticism when you stand up for yourself and affirm your own character and abilities whether others do or not.

In spite of criticism

Tom Wolfe, the American author and journalist, tells of an incident in London in 1894 when George Bernard Shaw's new play opened. At the end of the final act, the audience gave tremendous applause, resulting in curtain call after curtain call. Finally, they began to cry, "Author! Author!"

So, Shaw himself came onstage. He was a tall, pinch-shouldered man, according to Wolfe's account, with a beard-and-a-half and a long mustache. He walked to center stage while the audience generated even more intense applause.

Suddenly, amidst the applause and bravos, a loud voice shouted, "Boo! Booo! Boooo!"

The audience became silent and every head turned to see a man in the gallery, cupping his hands around his mouth like a megaphone. It was a young drama critic, bellowing out again, "Boo! Booo!"

As you can imagine, everyone was shocked, and all heads turned toward the stage and stared at Shaw, standing alone, the victim of this ambush. What would he say?

He was renowned for his wit, but who could be prepared for this kind of onslaught? When the young critic paused in his booing, Shaw looked up, smiled, and in a congenial voice, said, "My dear fellow, I quite agree with you. But what are we two against so many?"

The audience rose to its feet, applauded, cheered, and nearly raised the roof off the building with their thunderous response. Shaw had obviously uttered the right words at the right time.[3]

If I had been standing onstage, those are the words I would have wanted to say—but probably would not have thought of until the next day!

Many of us would have been thoroughly cowed by such a critic. Or angered. Or embarrassed. But to be able to handle it with humor and, in the process, speak words of self-affirmation is the mark of genius.

The problem many of us face, from the time we are children, is that we have a negative self-image or at least low self-esteem. We can blame our parents for the way they treated us or our teachers for regimenting the creativity out of us. But there's little to be gained by blaming others. The key is: what do we do about it?

(A word to parents: The more you can affirm your children, let them know you are proud of them, and encourage them to do their best without expecting perfection, the better you will prepare them for a mature and successful future. Children who grow up with criticism learn to criticize others. Those who grow up with affirmation are much more likely to develop self-confidence and in turn be affirming to others.)

At some point in life, we have to take responsibility for ourselves. No one else is going to do it, nor should they. Viktor Frankl, the Jewish psychologist from Vienna, spent time in a Nazi concentration camp during World War II. He said the Germans took him in a room and had him strip down to his bare skin. They laughed at him and mocked him. It was there and then that he determined they could take away everything he had but they could not take away from him the ability to choose his own attitude. He said, "Everything can be taken from a man but one thing: the last of the human freedoms—to choose one's attitude in any given set of circumstances, to choose one's own way."[4]

Making the choice to be a positive, self-affirming person goes a long way toward enabling you to accomplish your goals in life and encourage others while you do it. It is so important that we learn to be positive about ourselves. As Earl Nightingale said, "Show the world a poor attitude and you become a magnet for unpleasant experiences. Show a good attitude and you attract good experiences."[5]

In spite of circumstances

Some people have developed an attitude of self-affirmation in the face of very difficult circumstances. Roland Hayes was a humble and greatly gifted African-American tenor. He said,

> My voice teacher told me that as an artist, and as a black
> artist, I would suffer terribly and needlessly if I allowed the

barbs to penetrate my soul. But if my heart was right and my spirit divinely disciplined, then nobody in all of the world would be able to hurt me. I know now that this is true. I try every moment to live in such awareness of the presence of God that no bitterness can creep into my heart. In this way I have learned to be happy even in the discovery that nobody in the world can hurt me, except myself.[6]

Jill Kinmount was once a top female American downhill skier. In fact, she was the reigning national champion in the slalom. She fell and severed her spine in a race just before her twentieth birthday and became a quadriplegic. When she was forty-one, someone asked her what accounted for her bright and positive outlook on life. The questioner wondered if it was because she had nineteen great years in the beginning.

"I beg your pardon," she replied. "I've had forty-one great years."[7]

Jill had no choice about giving up the ability to walk. But she still had control over her attitude. And fortunately, she chose to be a self-affirming individual, which made her pleasant to be around instead of someone who spreads doom and gloom.

Francie Baltazar-Schwartz says Jerry was the guy you love to hate because he was always in a good mood and always spoke positively. If anyone asked him how he was doing, he would answer, "If I were any better, I would be twins."

He worked as a manager in the restaurant business and attracted a number of loyal employees who loved him because he was always so positive.

Francie asked him, "You can't be a positive person all the time. How do you do it?" He replied that he wakes up each morning and reminds himself he has two choices. He can choose to be in a good mood or a bad mood. He chooses to be in a good mood. If something bad happens, he can choose to be a victim or he can learn from it. He chooses to learn from it.

When challenged that it can't be that easy, Jerry says, "Yes, it is. Life is all about choices. You choose how you react to situations. It's your choice how you live your life."

One day Jerry did something you are never supposed to do in the restaurant business: he left the back door open and was held up by three armed robbers. Trying to open the safe, his hand was shaking and it slipped off the combination. One of the robbers panicked and shot him. Fortunately, he was found quickly and rushed to a trauma center. After eighteen hours of surgery and weeks of intensive care, he was released from the hospital with bullet fragments still in his body.

Six months after the accident, someone asked him what went through his mind as the robbery took place. He said he was thinking he should have locked the back door! But as he was lying on the floor, he remembered he had two choices: he could choose to live or choose to die. He chose to live.

When asked if he was scared, he said, "The paramedics were great. They kept telling me I was going to be fine. But when they wheeled me into the emergency room and I saw the expressions on the faces of the doctors and nurses, I got really scared. In their eyes, I read, 'He's a dead man.' I knew I needed to take action.

"A big, burly nurse was shouting questions at me. She asked if I was allergic to anything. 'Yes,' I replied. The doctors and nurses stopped working as they waited for my reply...I took a deep breath and yelled, 'Bullets!' Over their laughter, I told them, 'I am choosing to live. Operate on me as if I am alive, not dead!'"[8]

Jerry lived—certainly because of the doctors' skill, but also because of his powerful, positive attitude. We can all make the choice to live. An attitude of self-affirmation means I choose to live and be positive.

COMPLIMENT AND PRAISE OTHERS

As important as it is to engage in self-affirmation, it is equally important to affirm others. This is much easier for some people than for others. One of the first steps is to stop throwing barbs at others.

Stop throwing barbs

One of the reasons some of us find it difficult to praise others is that we're in the habit of expressing put-downs instead. John told me that years ago he used to say negative things to people in a joking way.

He didn't mean to be abusive or insulting. It was his way of being light-hearted. One day someone was taking pictures and John said, "Here, let me stand next to Phil. I feel much thinner when I stand here." John was overweight himself, but Phil outweighed him by forty or fifty pounds. John laughed nervously and glanced at Phil. The look on Phil's face told him it was not funny. In fact, he looked insulted.

John said, "It finally dawned on me how unfair it was to poke fun at others just to make me feel better about myself." John turned over a new leaf and learned to affirm instead of insult.

Make it short and positive

Your affirmations don't have to be long and involved. A simple observation about something the other person did or said can be very meaningful.

Joni Eareckson Tada is amazed at how her husband, Ken, responds to words of encouragement. She will say things like, "Ken, thank you for going to visit that neighbor who has cancer. That was a thoughtful thing to do."

She is not talking about flattery or smooth, sweet talk just to get something she wants. She is recommending that we make pronouncements and declarations of the good we see in others.

She says even letting them borrow something of value—like a favorite book, your car, or your fine china—are all ways to affirm your neighbor. "When you place something of value in the hands of another," she says, "it's a signal that you notice a virtue in the other person that elevates your confidence in her trustworthiness."

Why are words of encouragement and affirmation so important to Joni? Because she is limited in what she can do physically. She is a quadriplegic, the result of a diving accident when she was seventeen years old. Consequently, she can't whip up an omelet for her husband or rub his back. But, she says, "I can honor and uplift him with words that give life, hope, and encouragement."[9]

Put it in writing

Joni also recommends sending notes to people. Remembering what the ancient wise man said—"Worry weighs a person down; an encouraging word cheers a person up"[10]—she says a note of encouragement can be particularly meaningful. And especially to children. "You can't do better than affirm a child," she declares.

I have often recommended writing notes as a way to affirm others. And let's face it, a handwritten note has become a rarity. Even if your handwriting is not very legible, if people know it came from you, it leaves a lasting impression.

And don't wait for a holiday or even some specific event when such notes might be expected. A simple note that says, "I appreciate you," says volumes to the recipient. Ken Blanchard said, "The key to developing people is to catch them doing something right."[11] And of course let them know you noticed.

Applaud good work

In that same vein, Samuel Goldwyn, American film producer, said, "When someone does something good, applaud. You'll make two people happy."[12]

Skitch Henderson, the renowned musical conductor and founder of the New York Pops, said, "I watch the public like a hawk. If I see boredom, I worry. You can tell by the applause: There's perfunctory applause, there's light applause, and then there's real applause. When it's right, applause sounds like vanilla ice cream with chocolate sauce."[13]

Why is applause so important? It's letting the performers know they are appreciated. It's the audience's way of affirming the actors, singers, or other performers for a job well done.

Avoid taking others for granted

Everybody likes to be affirmed. Former Speaker of the House Tip O'Neill said an elderly neighbor came up to him after leaving the polls on election day and said, "Tip, I voted for you today even though you didn't ask me."

This caught O'Neill by surprise. "Mrs. O'Brien," he said, "I've known you all my life. I took your garbage out for you, mowed your lawn, shoveled snow for you. I didn't think I had to ask."

In a motherly tone, she said, "Tip, it's always nice to be asked."[14]

Asking—rather than taking people for granted—is another way of affirming people. It's letting them know they are important to you.

"Do not save your loving speeches for your friends till they are dead," said Anna Cummins. "Do not write them on their tombstones, speak them rather now instead."[15]

Keep it practical

What are some practical ways to affirm others? Here are a few:

1. At family gatherings, encourage everyone to name one thing they admire about a family member.

2. Affirm someone who is chronically ill for their patience and endurance.

3. Commend someone for being a problem solver, even without waiting to be asked to solve the problem. Affirm their initiative.

4. The next time someone points out an error you made, affirm them for bringing it to your attention.

5. Take time to affirm someone who is reliable or punctual.

6. When someone passes along a good idea, affirm them for their thoughtfulness.

7. If you are aware of someone who is especially humble, commend their humility to another person.

8. When one of your children (or someone else's child) brings up some positive insight they gained at school or in church, commend them for their attentiveness.

9. Affirm someone for their flexibility when you observe them changing their plans.

10. Affirm someone who makes do in disappointing circumstances.[16]

BE TACTFUL

Psyches are fragile. We need to handle them with care. This calls for tact.

A good start

Diane Sawyer is well-known as a television journalist who has had some impressive jobs. She was anchor of *ABC World News,* co-anchor of *Good Morning America,* and co-anchor of *Primetime* newsmagazine. But her highly successful career didn't start in a promising way. When she came home to Louisville, Kentucky, from college, she had no clear direction. She admits that at college she had spent four years majoring in identity crisis and self-absorption, with a minor in poetry and daydreaming.

So her father helped to get her jump-started by asking her three questions:

- What is it you love?
- Where is the most adventurous place you could do it?
- Are you certain it will serve other people?[17]

As she answered those questions, a direction became apparent to her. What did she love? She loved stories—writing them and telling them. She went to law school for a semester, but she realized she didn't want to litigate. Instead she wanted to just tell people, "You won't believe what happened in this case."

As for adventure, there were no women doing TV news reporting in Kentucky in those days, so she showed up at a local news station and offered to start anywhere. She started as a weather girl. The problem was she was nearsighted. Without her contact lenses, she couldn't see the West Coast of the map from where she was standing on the East Coast, so she was always taking wild guesses at the weather in San Francisco.

Then there was the night she signed off by saying, "The high temperature for today was seventy-eight degrees. Currently it's eighty-five."

In spite of her inauspicious start, she gradually worked her way into the newsroom and eventually to a national spot with ABC News. She says anytime someone has asked her for career advice, she has repeated those three questions her dad asked her. She says they are like one of those global positioning satellites. They will help you find your direction.

Those questions are a wonderful example of her father's tact. Of all the things he could have said to her when she came home from college, he chose words that launched her on a successful career. Think of what he might have said. He could have said, "You mean we spent all that money on a college degree and you don't know what you want to do?" Or he could have said, "It looks to me like you have wasted your time. Now what are you going to do?" Or he could have said, "You'd better get your act together, young lady, if you ever expect to amount to anything."

Instead he came up with three wonderful questions that both challenged her and affirmed her. He knew she had potential and he tactfully chose questions that would help to unlock that potential.

Where it all began

Tracing the origin of the word *tact* takes us back to the seventeenth century, where it came from the Latin *tactus*, which has to do with the sense of touch. From the same root we have the word *tactile*, which Merriam-Webster defines as "perceptible by touch: tangible." *Tact* came to mean skill in dealing with persons or sensitive situations. It has been defined as "intuitive perception, especially a quick and fine perception of what is fit and proper and right; a ready appreciation of the proper thing to do or say, especially a fine sense of how to avoid giving offense."[18]

Diplomats need tact as they often have to handle delicate issues and come to a compromise without giving away the farm and without giving offense to the other person. Tact recognizes the other person's rights and seeks a harmonious solution. It may involve putting oneself in the other person's shoes and looking at the problem from their perspective.

To mature in our use of tact, we need to understand that the same thing can be said in a tactful way or in an untactful manner. A shoe salesman tells a customer, "I'm sorry, madam, but your foot is too large for this shoe." Another salesman, in a similar situation, might say, "I'm sorry, madam, but this shoe is too small for your foot."[19]

You can see the value of using tact to put a situation in a different perspective, couching it in positive terms instead of negative, and possibly insulting, terms.

Unconsciously tactful

William Carey, the British missionary, was diplomatic without seeming to be conscious of his skill. Someone who knew him well said about him, "He has attained the happy art of ruling and overruling others without asserting his authority, or others feeling their subjection—and all is done without the least appearance of design on his part."[20]

What a great quality to have. To be able to persuade others, or even correct others if that needs to be done, and do it with grace calls for tact. Bob Burg says, "Tact is the language of strength. It is the ability to say something or make a point in such a way that not only is the other person not offended; they are totally receptive." He recommends, "Every situation you find yourself in, and every time you must call someone's attention to a particular way of acting, keep 'tact' in mind." From a practical standpoint, he suggests we ask ourselves questions such as, "How will he or she feel about what I'm about to say and how I'm about to say it?"[21]

USE POWER WORDS

Most of us don't realize how powerful our words are. We may be flippant or careless about using certain words and phrases, but here are three powerful phrases that we need to use often.

I love you

Smiley Blanton, an American psychiatrist, made this thought-provoking observation:

> To say that one will perish without love does not mean that everyone without adequate love dies. Many do, for without love the will to live is often impaired to such an extent that

a person's resistance is critically lowered and death follows. But most of the time, lack of love makes people depressed, anxious, and without zest for life. They remain lonely and unhappy, without friends or work they care for, their life a barren treadmill, stripped of all creative action and joy.[22]

A judge in Philadelphia dealt with many juveniles in trouble with the law. He said most young people who came into court were hostile and aggressive. But he was bothered more by the attitude of their parents. The parents seemed indignant that their children would be brought into court.

However, said the judge, "Never did I see any of those fathers show any affection for their teenagers. Never once did a father put his arm around his son or daughter. Never once did he even touch his child. When a parent shows love, even by a simple act of touching, there is an opportunity for redemption. Otherwise young people die emotionally, they die mentally because of a lack of love."[23]

But that's enough of negative examples. Here's a positive story to lift your spirits. After the devastating January 2010 earthquake in Haiti, the story came to light about Charity, one of 131 children who lived in an orphanage. Rescue workers found 130 children. Charity was missing. They searched all night and finally found her the next morning. She was trapped in a small space with barely enough room to breathe. The workers wanted to know, after they dug her out of the rubble, "Charity, what did you do while you were trapped there all those hours?"

She said, "I sang, 'Love lifted me. Love lifted me. When nothing else could help, love lifted me.'"[24]

In case you don't remember, that's an old gospel song that she had apparently heard. But it's exactly what happened. The loving hands of people reached out and lifted that precious girl. It was love in action.

And while that is wonderful and necessary, I want to establish the importance of saying, "I love you." Those are three of the most powerful words you can utter. Suppose the people in Smiley Blanton's observation had heard those power words. How might it have changed the whole course of their lives? What about the teens in that Philadelphia judge's court? What if those fathers, instead of angrily demanding to know why people were persecuting their children, had been saying to their sons and daughters regularly, "I love you"?

Henry Drummond said, "You will find, as you look back upon your life, that the moments when you really lived are the moments when you have done things in the spirit of love."[25]

Showing love and speaking love to others not only does powerful things for them, it also does powerful things for you as the one giving the love.

I forgive you

Here are three more powerful words. A friend once said, "If you haven't asked someone to forgive you in the past six months, you have either been perfect or proud."

Wow! That will take the starch out of your self-righteousness!

But just as we need to ask for forgiveness, we also need to offer forgiveness freely.

A father in Spain had a strained relationship with his teenage son, and the young man ran away from home. Soon the father began to search for him. Although he looked in many places, he was unsuccessful. Finally, in Madrid, he made one last desperate gesture. He put an ad in the newspaper. The ad read: "Dear Paco, meet me in front of the newspaper office at noon. All is forgiven. I love you. Your father."

At noon the next day, in front of the newspaper office, eight hundred "Pacos" showed up. They all sought forgiveness and love from their fathers.[26]

Truth be told, nearly everyone we meet could profit by sitting down with someone and either seeking or giving forgiveness.

Forgiving others can be difficult. A couple of common ideas about forgiveness may help to make it less difficult. One is the idea of "forgiving and forgetting." We think if we forgive, we must forget what the offending person did. Only God has the ability to do that. Through Isaiah, God said, "I am he who blots out your transgressions…and remembers your sins no more" (Isaiah 43:25).

Does God have amnesia? Does God truly forget? God knows

everything, so it is better if we think of it this way: When God forgives, he treats us *as if* he does not remember. He will not hold it against us ever again.

Others have trouble forgiving because we think it isn't right to let the other person off the hook for what they did. Forgiveness is not pretending something bad didn't happen. The one who forgives is fully aware of what happened but chooses to let go and give up the right to get even.

Corrie ten Boom, who survived the German concentration camp at Ravensbrück, compares forgiveness to letting go of a bell rope. Have you ever rung an old-fashioned bell in a steeple? If so you know that sometimes you have to tug a bit to get it started ringing. Once it begins, as long as you keep pulling on the rope, the bell will continue to ring. When you take your hands off the rope, the bell will slow and eventually stop.

Ten Boom said, "When we forgive someone, we take our hand off the rope. But if we've been tugging at our grievances for a long time, we mustn't be surprised when the old angry thoughts keep coming up for a while. They're just the *ding-dongs* of the old bell slowing down."[27]

Forgiveness is not based on feeling. It is something you choose to do. But the good news is: "The farther you walk in forgiveness, the greater the distance you put between yourself and the negative situation."[28]

I am proud of you

We would probably be amazed to know the low percentage of children who hear from their parents, "I'm proud of you." I don't have any statistics on it. It's just a sense I have from talking with people that it's more uncommon than we would like to think. A child who grows up hearing "I'm proud of you" spoken sincerely by a parent has a better chance of success in this world.

But what about adults? How can we say, "I am proud of you," without sounding smarmy or ingratiating?

Tim Madigan, a journalist for the *Fort Worth Star-Telegram*, wrote a book describing his friendship with Fred Rogers of public television's *Mr. Rogers' Neighborhood*. He first met Mr. Rogers in 1995 when he traveled from Texas to Pittsburgh to profile him for his newspaper. Their meeting also coincided with a season in which Madigan was wrestling with a number of personal issues: profound depression, complex feelings about his father, and the catastrophic illness of his younger brother. Over the following months, through emails, phone calls, and personal visits, Madigan began to share his personal concerns with Mr. Rogers.

Fred Rogers responded with what Madigan could only call "supernatural love, wholly without judgment, and with perfect clarity, wisdom, and compassion." Mr. Rogers would say, "Anything mentionable is manageable."

But then came December 1997, when Madigan and his wife were about to split up. He was concerned about how to tell their two children, how to tell their parents, how he could afford an apartment, and how he could tell Fred Rogers, who had devoted his life to children and their families. Could Mr. Rogers forgive a man who was destroying his own family?

The answer came in a two-page, handwritten letter:

> *My dear Tim,*
>
> *Bless your heart. I feel so for you—for you all—but, Tim, please know that I would never forsake you, that I will never be disappointed with you, that I would never stop loving you. How I wish we could be closer geographically! I'd get in my car, drive to your house, knock on your door, and, when you answered I'd hug you tight… You write of "powerlessness." Join the club, we are not in control: God is.*
>
> *Our trust and affection run deep. You know you are in my prayers—now and always. If you ever need me you only have to call and I would do my best to get to you or you to me…*
>
> *You are my beloved brother, Tim. You are God's beloved son.*[29]

Although Fred Rogers did not use the words, "I am proud of you," in that letter, he transmitted the same ideas of love, acceptance, and support that such a phrase communicates.

Saying "I am proud of you" to another adult may seem perfectly appropriate. Or in some cases you may want to use other words:

"You amaze me."

"Way to go!"

"Sweet!"

"Outstanding job."

"You are a rock star!"

To your spouse, you might even give the phrase a different twist: "I'm so proud to be your husband [or wife]."

All of us can use positive word power and become more proficient in it as we learn and grow. Rising out of a positive attitude, let's learn to practice self-affirmation. Let's become more consistent in complimenting and praise others. With practice, we can become more tactful. And we can learn to use power words of love, forgiveness, and pride to build up others.

Chapter Ten

NEGATIVE WORD POWER

Even the best strategy can be foiled or undermined, so
you must guard against having a negative attitude by
choosing words that are not destructive. In this chapter,
you will learn four ways to rid your life of negative speech:
(1) Avoid idle talk, gossip, and needless arguments, (2)
eliminate insults and innuendo, (3) hold your tongue,
and (4) banish "red" words (profanity and slurs).

*"If you keep on saying things are going to be bad,
you have a good chance of being a prophet."*

ISAAC SINGER[1]

David Aikman tells the story of George W. Bush when he was at Yale University. One morning late in 1964, young George introduced himself to the chaplain at the university, William Sloan Coffin. It was after Bush senior, himself a Yale alumnus, had been defeated by Ralph Yarborough in a run for a senate seat in Texas. George W. had been deeply hurt by his father's loss. When Bush met the chaplain, the minister said, "Oh, yes, I know your father. Frankly, he was beaten by the better man."

Years later, Coffin apologized for this unkind remark. But Barbara Bush, George W.'s mother, believed this remark by the chaplain kept George W. away from church at Yale and probably helped turn him away from organized religion for quite a while. It was obviously a case of the wrong words at the wrong time.[2]

A negative attitude produces negative words. Those words take many forms. Some are hurtful. Some are unkind. Others are insulting. Some are profane. Whatever form they take, we can improve our reputations and our helpfulness to others by eliminating negative expressions.

It's possible to gain a reputation—for good or bad—based on the way we talk. Norman Vincent Peale was known as the father of positive thinking. His book, *The Power of Positive Thinking*, was published in 1952, and Peale's popularity skyrocketed. Some people loved him because of his positive emphasis on life, while others were skeptical.

Adlai Stevenson, governor of Illinois and two-time presidential candidate, was invited to give a speech before a religious convention during the 1956 campaign. Stevenson's host remarked that the candidate had been invited as a courtesy and that Norman Vincent Peale had already encouraged attendees at the convention to vote for Dwight D. Eisenhower. Stevenson quipped, "Speaking as a Christian, I find the Apostle Paul appealing and the Apostle Peale appalling."[3]

Nevertheless, Peale had the reputation of being extremely positive. When he and his wife were traveling in Europe, their hosts gave them a room with an ancient bed. At least the headboard was ancient, with the date "1620" boldly engraved in it. Peale sat on the edge of the bed, looked at the headboard, and said to his wife, "Think of how many people have died in this bed."

Ruth Stafford Peale said, "Norman, that's the trouble with you—you're too negative. Think of all the people who have been born in that bed!"

I suppose even the most positive people have the occasional lapse. The real issue is how to keep from being sidetracked by our own negative attitudes and negative talk.

AVOID IDLE TALK

Some idle talk is intended as harmful. Some of it is just poorly thought through. For instance, in 1927, when talking pictures were just coming on screen, Harry Warner, the president of Warner Brothers, asked whether people would want to hear actors talk. Or take Robert

Millikan, the Nobel Prize winner in physics in 1923. He said, "There is no likelihood man can ever tap the power of the atom." Here's one you'll love, from Charles Duell, head of the US Patent Office. In 1899 he said, "Everything that can be invented, has been invented."[4]

What did all three of those gentlemen have in common? Besides uttering idle talk, they were just plain dead wrong. But more importantly, their foolish statements came from negative thinking. Instead of thinking possibilities, they were thinking impossibilities. Negative thinking drags you down. And what does it do to your own future? As the Isaac Singer quote at the beginning of this chapter implies, your negative thinking and negative words could become a self-fulfilling prophecy.

Rumors

Rumors are easy to start and difficult to stop. Psychologists have conducted many experiments—and you may have even played it as a party game—where A tells B that a red pickup truck ran a stop sign. B repeats the story to C and so on down the line, until by the time Z hears it, a semi has mowed down a pack of Scouts.

Carl Jung, the pioneering psychiatrist, discovered this very principle at work in a case study at a girls' school. The rumor mill cranked out a steamy story about a teacher and a student who were having an affair. The fact was that the student had an erotic dream about the teacher and told the dream to three friends. From there the story was told and retold until the dream became "fact."[5]

Jung's experiment took place in 1910. What may have taken a day or two to make its way around the campus could now travel around the world in seconds. Rumors swirl around politicians, celebrities, and companies, as well as ordinary people. To make matters worse, stories may be told in our 24/7 news cycle before facts are thoroughly checked. If the story turns out to be false, the news outlet just retracts it and moves on.

Fred Koenig, a psychology professor at Tulane University in New Orleans, advised companies who were the victims of rumor "to immediately and publicly deny the rumor as untrue and without a shred of substantiation." He recommended scheduling a press conference and offering "a substantial reward for any information leading to the arrest and conviction of the person behind the rumor." He predicted the person would never be found and the reward would go unpaid, but going public puts an end to the rumor by "transforming it into news. Once it's news, the motivation for the little guy to spread the story to get attention is dramatically reduced."[6]

What's the difference between rumors and gossip? Koenig says gossip is "about people you know" and "rumors are about people you don't know personally and about large institutions."

Gossip

Gossip is one of the more insidious forms of negative talk. The ancient wise man said, "The words of a gossip are like choice morsels; they go down to the inmost parts."[7] Playing off the "choice morsels" simile, someone developed a recipe for "Sinfully Rich Choice Morsels: A Recipe for Delicious Gossip." Here are the ingredients:

> 1 cup pride
> ¾ cup hearsay
> ½ cup evil suspicion
> ¼ cup grumbling
> 1 tablespoon bitterness
> ¾ tablespoon slander
> 2 teaspoons yeast of exaggeration
> 3 teaspoons sharing the situation
> Pinch of flattery
> Dash of unfaithfulness
>
> Directions: Mix together all ingredients in a bowl of betrayal. Pour into a medium saucepan and bring to a boil, stirring constantly. Prepare in a dark kitchen. Turn on low and simmer overnight. Sprinkle with the truth (optional). Serve hot to itching ears, warm to those not minding their own business, and cold to those who are fearful.[8]

You know better than to gossip, right? But what about those who want to gossip to you? How do you deal with that?

Change the subject. If you bring up another subject, maybe it will distract the gossiper from continuing in a negative vein. If the conversation isn't going in the direction you want it to go, you may need to be proactive in shifting the direction.

Be positive about the target of the gossip. If you know of something good the target has said or done, be quick to speak about the positive contributions that person has made. It's harder for a gossip to be negative when the person they're talking about has just been shown to be a good role model.

Confront gossip politely but firmly. Just tell the person who is talking that you aren't interested in hearing that story. You may be able to confront by saying, "That sounds like gossip to me. Let's change the subject." Your conversation partner will get the point.

Point out incomplete information. A good deal of gossip deals in half-truths. It contains just enough truth to be palatable, but not enough to reveal the whole story. Just because we hear a story doesn't necessarily make it true. Point out that it doesn't sound like the person you know, it isn't true to her character, or whatever you can honestly say.

Turn the gossip into a prayer. How much better if we talk to God about the person instead of talking to other people.[9]

Mother Theresa recommended the following ways to practice humility, which will certainly help us avoid gossip:

> To speak as little as possible of one's self. To mind one's own business. Not to want to manage other people's affairs. To avoid curiosity. To accept contradictions and correction cheerfully. To pass over the mistakes of others. To accept insults and injuries. To accept being slighted, forgotten and disliked. To be kind and gentle even under provocation. Never to stand on one's dignity. To choose always the hardest.[10]

Arguments

Discussion is one thing. Being argumentative is another. Having a conversation in which two people disagree with each other is not necessarily an argument. It may just be a healthy discussion in which you exchange opinions. On the other hand, some people are argumentative. They love to argue, even about trivial things, just to be different. Their goal seems to be to engage others in verbal sparring matches.

How do you deal with them? Dr. Nicola Davies suggests: "People who constantly argue seek control and power over others. You cannot reason with them, so it's best to withdraw from an argument than try to prove them wrong."[11]

The old saying, "It takes two to argue," is true. Walk away if necessary. Needless arguments are a waste of time.

ELIMINATE INSULTS AND INNUENDOS

Insults can take many forms, from rudeness to slights to disparaging remarks to outright slander. Or sometimes you meet that rare individual who might be tempted to act rudely but who responds in an unexpected way.

Insults

Tony Campolo tells about a friend of his who was shopping at Nordstrom department store in Bel Air, a wealthy neighborhood in Los Angeles, California. It was during the Christmas season when she enjoyed the magnificent Christmas decorations, even if she couldn't afford to buy anything.

On one of her visits, she was looking at some fine—and expensive—dresses on the top floor. The elevator opened and a bag lady stepped out. Her clothes were dirty and her stockings were rolled down to her ankles. She held a gym bag in one hand. She was obviously out of place and could not buy anything. The dresses, after all, were in the thousand-dollar category.

Tony's friend expected a security guard to arrive any minute and usher the disheveled woman out of the store. Instead, a stately saleswoman approached her and asked, "May I help you, madam?"

"Yeah," she answered, "I wanna buy a dress."

"What kind of dress?" the saleswoman asked politely.

"A party dress!"

"You've come to the right place," said the saleswoman. "Follow me. I think we have some of the finest party dresses in the world."

The saleswoman then proceeded to spend more than ten minutes matching dresses with the woman's skin color and eye color, trying to help her determine which dress would go best with her complexion. After selecting three dresses that seemed to be most appropriate for the bag lady, she invited the woman to follow her into the dressing room.

Tony's friend hurried into the adjoining dressing room and put her ear to the wall. She wanted to hear all of this, because it was so remarkable.

The bag lady tried on the dresses, with assistance from the saleswoman. After about ten minutes, the bag lady said abruptly, "I've changed my mind. I'm not going to buy a dress today!"

The saleswoman answered gently, "That's okay. But here's my card. Should you come back to Nordstrom department store, I do hope you will ask for me. I would consider it such a privilege to wait on you again."

Tony observed, "This, of course, is a brilliant illustration of what Jesus would do, if Jesus was a saleswoman at Nordstrom."[12]

It's also a beautiful example of how to turn a situation fraught with negative possibilities into one that expresses kindness rather than insult. I can imagine a less graceful and polished salesperson might have been abrupt with the bag lady, might have refused to wait on her, might have called for security to escort her out of the store. In so many ways, she could have belittled, berated, and insulted the poor woman. Instead, she treated her with dignity.

Og Mandino said, "Beginning today, treat everyone you meet, friend or foe, loved one or stranger, as if they were going to be dead at midnight. Extend to each person you meet, no matter how trivial the contact, all the care and the kindness and understanding and love that you can muster, and do it with no thought of any reward."[13]

Responding to insults

What if you are the target of an insult? Dr. Neel Burton suggests five ways to respond:

Anger. This is the weakest response because (1) it shows you take the insult, and perhaps the insulter, seriously; (2) it suggests there may be truth in the insult; and (3) it shows you are upset, which may invite further insults.

Acceptance. Although this seems weak, it may be the strongest response. If you respect the person who insulted you, you may want to take what they say seriously and profit from any truth. If the insulter is unworthy of consideration, take it in the same spirit you would a barking dog, in which case you have no reason to take offense.

Returning the insult. This is not a good idea as it brings you down to the level of the insulter and tends to elevate him or her to your level.

Humor. This may be effective as it tends to undermine the insult, bring the audience (if any) to your side, and diffuses the tension. You may want to extend the insult: "Ah, if you had only known me better, you might have found greater fault."

Ignoring the insult. Humor requires quick thinking, while ignoring the insult is easier. It minimizes the insult by not taking it seriously.

Burton's conclusion is golden: "We need never take offense at an insult. Offense exists not in the insult but in our reaction to it, and our reactions are completely within our control."[14]

Innuendo

Innuendo may be defined as "an indirect or a subtle observation about a thing or a person. It is generally critical, disparaging, or salacious in nature, and its use is almost always derogatory."[15]

Without actually accusing someone of wrongdoing, it may be implied by the way a question is asked. The classic example is: "When did you stop beating your wife?" The person on the hot seat may never have beaten his wife, but the question implies that he has. The only concern is when did he stop.

The story is told of an old sailing ship, on which the first mate often became drunk. The captain warned him if it happened again, the offense would be recorded in the ship's log. Before long, it happened again, so the captain kept his word and wrote indelibly in the ship's log, "Tuesday, March 14, First Mate Drunk."

This hurt the old sailor and he vowed to take vengeance. Two days later, he slipped into the captain's quarters and wrote indelibly in the ship's log: "Thursday, March 16, Captain Sober Today."

A true statement, but by innuendo, it implied that on other days the captain was not sober.

Anyone wanting to improve his speech and master the art of being positive will avoid innuendo. Mean what you say and say what you mean without being derogatory about the other person, even by implication.

HOLD YOUR TONGUE

Johnathan Kana claims to have been stung by a Texas bull nettle, that perennial herb covered with stinging hairs. That's why he viciously chops down any that spring up in his yard. The plant's hairs are needle-sharp and cause a painful allergic reaction. A casual brush against it can lead to hours of pain. He says people who forage for the nettle's seeds declare they are delicious. But of course, that means being willing to brave the dangers of handling the plant.[16]

Unfortunately, our tongues can be equally dangerous. They can inflict the stinging of gossip, criticism, and other offensive remarks. Interesting thing about the Texas bull nettle: it displays beautiful white flowers in the early summer. In a similar way, the tongue can be an instrument that blesses and encourages others.

Maybe that's why an anonymous writer suggested the difference between a successful career and a mediocre one sometimes consists of leaving about four or five things a day unsaid.

Public speakers, who make their living using their tongue, are often at risk of misusing it. The story is told somewhere about an American Indian who went to church. It soon became obvious to him that the preacher was not well-prepared. To compensate for his lack of depth and preparation, the minister increased the volume of his voice and pounded the pulpit. After the service, someone asked the Native American what he thought of the message. The laconic Indian summed it up this way: "High wind. Big thunder. No rain."

Careless speech

It isn't just public speakers who get themselves into trouble with their tongues. A friend's mother had some traditional values, and she stopped him in his tracks one day. As a fourteen-year-old, he glanced at the clock and suddenly gulped down the rest of his dinner, trying to make a quick exit from the dinner table. Pushing back his chair, he said, "O God, it's late!"

His mother looked up from her plate, gave him a piercing glare, and said, "Don't you ever let me hear you say that again!"

"Mom, that's not swearing!"

She calmly corrected him: "It's taking God's name in vain, and we don't do that."

His mother was no theologian, but she did care about the way her son used his tongue.

Abraham Lincoln was entertaining a man one day who coaxed one of Lincoln's sons to sit on his lap. To entice him, he promised to give him the charm he wore on his watch chain. With that kind of promise, the child climbed up onto the man's lap.

When the man rose to go, Mr. Lincoln said, "Are you going to keep your promise to my boy?"

"What promise?"

"You said you would give him that charm."

"Oh, I could not. It is not only valuable, but I prize it as an heirloom."

"Give it to him," Lincoln said sternly. "I would not want him to know I entertained one who had no regard for his word."[17]

What comes out of our mouths

We can use our tongues for good or for evil, for positive purposes or negative purposes. The biblical writer James observed that "out of the same mouth come praise and cursing." He went on to say, "Can both fresh water and salt water flow from the same spring? My brothers and sisters, can a fig tree bear olives, or a grapevine bear figs? Neither can a salt spring produce fresh water" (James 3:10-12).

James was pointing out the problem of two opposite things coming from the same mouth. A fresh water spring gives fresh water because that's what's there. A fig tree bears figs because that's the kind of tree it is. What comes out of our mouths depends on what's in our minds and hearts. Somebody said, "It isn't the things that go in one ear and out the other that hurt as much as the things that go in one ear, get all mixed up, and then slip out the mouth." Sooner or later the character on the inside produces the speech that appears on the outside.

It reminds me of the young man who got on a subway train in New York City carrying a bull fiddle. The train was crowded, and he pushed his way along with his awkward baggage. Three persons he jostled muttered profanities and settled back into the gloom. But one lady who got bumped said, "Son, when you get to where you're going with that thing, I certainly hope they ask you to play."[18]

She could have muttered and cursed as the others did. But she controlled her tongue and managed to say something kind.

The ancient wise man, in his instructions designed to help us be wise, had many things to say about the tongue. For instance, "Whoever derides their neighbor has no sense, but the one who has understanding holds their tongue" (Proverbs 11:12).

Here's another: "The words of the reckless pierce like swords, but the tongue of the wise brings healing" (Proverbs 12:18).

And another: "Even fools are thought wise if they keep silent, and discerning if they hold their tongues" (Proverbs 17:28).

One more: "Those who guard their mouths and their tongues keep themselves from calamity" (Proverbs 21:23).

In the movie *Tomorrowland*, an interaction between the father and daughter shows her reminding him of a story he had told her many times. She says: "There are two wolves who are always fighting. One is darkness and despair. The other is light and hope. The question is…which wolf wins?" The father responds, "The one you feed." This is an old Cherokee parable that has been passed down, through story, for generations.[19]

What does that have to do with the tongue? It's another way to think about the fresh spring and the salt spring mentioned by James. It's a way to examine our inner reservoir from which our words come.

Taming the tongue

Be wise. Control the tongue. Here are five brief ways to tame your tongue:[20]

1. *Pause each morning.* Think about your day and how you want your words to affect others.

2. *Develop an awareness of your words.* As someone has said, "Taste your words before you spit them out."

3. *Surrender your "right" to complain.* Most people don't want to hear your complaints, and speaking about them only entrenches those negative ideas.

4. *Apologize for any unkind words you have spoken.* You cannot "un-say" the words, but you can acknowledge that they hurt the person to whom you were speaking.

5. *Practice speaking words that uplift and encourage.* That way everyone profits from your being around them. They won't cringe when they see you coming.

NO BARKING!

Profanity and open microphones are incompatible. Politicians who haven't learned to curb their swearing have been caught in the act and inadvertently recorded their obscenities for posterity.

Some people use shock words, says George LaMore Jr., "the way a Pekingese uses its big bark to bluff its way through life."[21] Both Republicans and Democrats have been caught barking on camera.

Profanity may be defined as using sacred or precious words to make cheap comparisons, cursing, or getting attention. Burgess Johnson said that swearing "seldom reflects a richness of invocation, but simply a poverty of vocabulary."[22] People who swear usually have one or two shock words they use. A person using profanity has been compared to a banjo with only one string.

Even to bring up the subject of public profanity makes one subject to the charge of being prudish. After all, everybody's using bad language these days, right?

Movie and TV standards

Perhaps the most prominent place we see moral standards slipping is in movies and TV shows. Language and content that were once considered unacceptable have become more and more mainstream. Hollywood continues to push the envelope. As pointed out in chapter 2 of this book, L. Brent Brozell III, the chair of the Parents Television Council in Los Angeles, has observed, "It's like an itch that can't be scratched enough," he says, "forever pushed to the next level."[23]

I read somewhere that the people who worked on the movie *Fly Away Home* admitted, "The studio didn't want a G-rated movie, even if it is a kids' movie. Kids don't go to G movies. So we had to put in some swear words. We planted those. A G-rating is the kiss of death."[24]

How often have you heard someone, reporting on a movie they had seen, say, "It was a good movie, great story line, excellent acting, but…" and you know what's coming, don't you? "But the language was really foul!"

"The 'F word,' long taboo, is now high fashion," observed Anya Bateman.[25] People excuse it by saying, "It's the real world. It's how people talk."

Consequently, our culture is experiencing an expletive explosion, a torrential downpour of language pollution. "Many people," says John W. Kennedy, "not just conservative Christians, see rampant swearing as part of an overall breakdown in civilization."[26]

Most parents and teachers will reprimand their children for swearing. Sometimes adults are corrected by spouses and coworkers. However, as Robert W. Peters, general counsel and president emeritus of Morality in Media, pointed out, there is a double standard between television and real life. "You never see stars embarrassed for swearing in a sitcom," he observed. "It's always 'funny.'"[27]

Influence on the job

James O'Connor, who runs a public relations firm, wrote *Cuss Control: The Comp Book on How to Curb Your Cursing*. He declares, "Swearing is a habit that comes out of laziness. It does influence the way people perceive your character, intelligence and maturity. To swear in public places is very abrasive and shows a lack of civility." He asks, "Do you want people to perceive you as rude, crude and cross or someone who is polite, mature and able not to cuss at every little irritation?"[28]

What some people don't seem to understand is that swearing is not commonly accepted in all situations. Wise employers know that it isn't just judging a person by their looks that can be risky. Their words say a great deal about them as well. One business manager told about a job applicant who came to an interview "dressed for success." He also had the background and training suitable for the job for which he was interviewing. So why wasn't he hired? The manager said, "If he felt no qualms about using expletives in our interview, he'd probably use them with our customers."[29]

But what if you have an employee or a coworker who is already working for you or with you and they use bad language? After all, many people don't take kindly to criticism. One secretary managed to speak to her boss about his profanity in a way that turned a criticism into a compliment. She told her boss, "I think so highly of you that it always surprises me when I hear you use bad language. I can't help feeling concerned about the impression you may be making on others who don't know you as well as I do."

The boss later admitted that no amount of blunt criticism would have had as purging an effect as his secretary's caring words.[30]

It's not really swearing

Some people use the cop-out that the Ten Commandments forbid taking God's name in vain but not other forms of swearing. If that's all the Bible said on the subject, we might agree. But Jesus reminded us that "the mouth speaks what the heart is full of" (Matthew 12:34). And the apostle Paul said, "Do not let any unwholesome talk come out of your mouths, but only what is helpful for building others up according to their needs, that it may benefit those who listen" (Ephesians 4:29).

On the back of a toothpaste box, you may find words like these: "[This product] can be of significant value when used in a conscientiously applied program of oral hygiene." From my perspective, we need a conscientiously applied program of moral oral hygiene and to curb the barking!

In addition to making you more pleasant to be around, it will put a sparkle in your mouth.

YOUR MOST IMPORTANT CONVERSATION

Your most important conversation is the one
you have with the Person who knows you better
than anyone, your heavenly Father.

We have spent a lot of words in this book talking about words. Although I have made occasional references to the Scriptures, I have not made this a strongly religious book. However, I would be remiss if I did not tell you about the most important conversation any of us could ever have. It's the conversation with our heavenly Father, the one Person in all the universe who knows us better than we even know ourselves.

I did not have what anyone would call an impressive start in life. I spent the early part of my childhood in a coal-mining community called Baileysville, West Virginia. A small town of fewer than one hundred people, its main street was more of a cul-de-sac than an actual street. But in Baileysville, we could see the majestic hills of West Virginia, as well as an old-fashioned swinging bridge over which we could cross the Guyandotte River.

Our family lived in a small three-room house on the side of Baileysville Mountain. My mother, my father, my two brothers, Mark and Terry, and I didn't have a lot, but we had each other. We fetched our water from a nearby well, and in the winter, our hardworking potbellied stove kept us warm. It ran on the same coal my father mined. We didn't have the luxury of a bathroom, but we did have a well-worn path to the outhouse. Nevertheless, it was home and we liked it.

One Saturday, we came home from our weekly excursion to the Wyoming County Store to find our home completely engulfed in flames. The house was too far gone to save and soon it was a pile of smoldering ashes.

My dad was a man of faith. His faith in the face of our hardships made a tremendous impression on my brothers and me. His faith helped to provide a firm foundation for the lives we have lived as adults. He had a profoundly positive attitude, even in the midst of tragedy. He was singularly focused on God. Although I cried for days after the fire destroyed our house, my father never wavered. He always knew that God would take care of us.

But as important as my father was to the development of my faith, my heavenly Father's influence has been even more important. My parents taught us early in our lives that we should have our own relationship with God. As devout as they were, it was not enough for us to ride on their coattails, so to speak. We needed to develop our own faith in a living God.

That's where this conversation I mentioned earlier comes into play. We learned from our parents, and it was reinforced in our church, that every person is accountable for his or her own life and each of us must have that all-important conversation with God.

I did go forward in our church—because that's just the way it was done in those days and in our culture. I went forward and knelt at an altar, and asked God to forgive me of my sins and to come into my life.

But this conversation can take place anywhere, anytime because God is always listening. He is always available to have this conversation.

To have this conversation and to begin a personal relationship with God is as simple as ABC.

Admit

We must admit that what the Bible says about us is true. It says, "All have sinned and fall short of the glory of God" (Romans 3:23). That simply means we have all done things we know are wrong, and we have failed to do things we know are right. I have known people who had a difficult time admitting they were sinners. But God has not singled you out as an extraordinarily bad person. Everyone has sinned.

When the writer says we have fallen short of the glory of God, he is simply stating what we know to be true: we have fallen short of God's ideal for us. God wants us to live a life that honors him and is pleasing in his sight.

Believe

One of my favorite Bible characters, the apostle Paul, had an adventure-filled life. On one of his missionary trips, he found himself in jail in a place called Philippi. Paul and his friend Silas had been falsely accused and although they were innocent, they had been severely beaten. They were placed in jail in chains with their feet in stocks. At midnight, however, the jail shook, the doors flew open, and their chains fell off. When the jailer saw this, knowing that he might face the death penalty for allowing prisoners to escape, he was ready to kill himself. But Paul urged him not to harm himself. The prisoners were all still there.

The jailer asked, "What must I do to be saved?"

Paul answered, "Believe in the Lord Jesus, and you will be saved—you and your household" (Acts 16:31).

That was good advice for the jailer and it's excellent advice for us. We too must believe on the Lord Jesus Christ. We must believe that Jesus died on the cross for our sins, and when we put our faith in what he did, God accepts his death as payment for our sins and forgives us of all the wrong things we have ever done.

Sound too good to be true? I know. But it is true. And by faith, we accept the gift of forgiveness God offers to us.

Confess

Another important element in beginning this relationship with God is confessing our sins. The word *confess* means "to agree with." So we agree with what the Bible says about us—that we are sinners. And we confess that we cannot save ourselves. No matter how many good things we do, we can never do enough to make up for the sins we have committed. God has made it simple for us. He says, "If we confess our sins, he is faithful and just and will forgive us our sins and purify us from all unrighteousness" (1 John 1:9).

In this all-important conversation with God, we confess our sins. We don't have to confess them to another human being. We must confess them to God. He is the one who can forgive us and give us eternal life.

Perhaps you have never prayed to God before and are not sure how to begin. Here is a simple prayer you can pray from your heart:

> *Dear God, I know I am a sinner. I'm sorry for my sins. Please come into my heart, forgive me of my sins, and help me to be the person you want me to be. I can't do it without your help, but I am willing to change. I am trusting you to forgive me. In Jesus's name, Amen.*

If you prayed that prayer from your heart, you have every right to believe that Jesus came into your heart and forgave you.

There's a wonderful Scripture that helps us understand what God does for us when we confess and invite him to come into our lives. John said, "And this is the testimony: God has given us eternal life, and this life is in his Son. Whoever has the Son has life; whoever does not have the Son of God does not have life" (1 John 5:11-12).

Jesus is the Son of God. If you have asked him to come into your life, you have eternal life. That's what those verses are assuring us is true. Eternal life means, among other things, that when you die, you go to heaven. In response to that prayer, Jesus not only comes into your life and forgives your sins, he also gives you eternal life, assurance of going to heaven someday.

You see why we say this is the most important conversation you can have. Of all the words you will ever say and all the conversations you will ever have, this is the one conversation you don't want to miss. It is a conversation with eternal consequences.

After you pray the prayer and claim the assurance, I encourage you to get involved in a Bible-believing church, one that will help you grow in your faith and help you to become a fully devoted follower of Jesus. Remember that a relationship with your heavenly Father is your privilege, now that you have received him into your life. Like every other relationship in your life, it must be cultivated. Reading your Bible daily will help. Daily prayer will help. Developing Christian friends will help. But your commitment to follow through with all your heart is extremely important.

God bless you as you grow to become more like Christ with each passing day.

Stan Toler

ENDNOTES

CHAPTER 1—WORDS CREATE

1. Yehuda Berg, accessed March 26, 2018, www.huffingtonpost.com/dr-hyder-zahed/the-power-of -spoken-words_b_6324786.html.

2. Marlo Thomas, *The Right Words at the Right Time* (New York: Atria Books, 2002), 217-18.

3. Genesis 1:3.

4. Jennifer Merin, "Experts Share Their Gift of Gab," *USA Today*, May 18, 1999.

5. Merin, "Experts Share Their Gift of Gab." The quotations from Eileen Ford, Malachy Court, and Jerry Falwell all came from Merin's article.

6. "Quote Fancy," accessed March 17, 2018, https://quotefancy.com/quote/19703/Henry-Ford-The -man-who-thinks-he-can-and-the-man-who-thinks-he-can-t-are-both-right-Which.

7. Mouse brain info: Carl Zimmer, "Secrets of the Brain," *National Geographic*, accessed March 18, 2018, https://gagueira.files.wordpress.com/2014/04/gagueira-national-geographic-fev-2014 -secrets-of-the-brain.pdf.

8. No one seems to know for sure where this wolf parable originated. Some say the Cherokee Indians, others attribute it to evangelist Billy Graham, still others to Irish playwright George Bernard Shaw.

9. Paul J. Meyer, accessed March 18, 2018, www.brainyquote.com/quotes/paul_j_meyer_188704.

10. Lee Strobel, *God's Outrageous Claims* (Grand Rapids, MI: Zondervan, 1997), 133.

11. Paul White quote: "The 5 Languages of Appreciation in the Workplace," *Outcomes*, Summer 2011, 43.

12. Cited by Strobel, *God's Outrageous Claims*, 128-29.

13. Les Parrott III, "Know Thyself," *Rev!*, March/April 2000, 31.

14. Leonard Sweet, "Being Right or Being in a Relationship," *Rev!*, September/October 2003, 17.

15. Attributed to Ann Landers, accessed March 28, 2018, www.resonancecontent.com/blog/ann -landers-content-marketing-genius/.

16. Ecclesiastes 3:1-2,7.

17. Job 1–2.

18. Hans Finzel, *The Top Ten Mistakes Leaders Make* (Wheaton, IL: Victor Books, 1994), 57.

19. John Ortberg, *Everybody's Normal Until You Get to Know Them* (Grand Rapids, MI: Zondervan, 2003), title page.

20. Tom Peters, "A Handwritten Thank-You Always Welcome," *Chicago Tribune*, accessed March 20, 2018, http://articles.chicagotribune.com/1995-02-20/business/9502200192_1_network -building-for-years-tiniest-personal-touch-pithy-personal-notes.

21. Norman Vincent Peale, "Image Your Way to Confidence," *PLUS*, July/August 2000, 16.

22. Bobb Biehl, *Dream Energy* (Quick Wisdom Publishing, 2001), 155.

23. Fred Smith, *Learning to Lead* (Dallas: Word Publishing, 1986), 168.

24. Cited by John C. Maxwell, *The 21 Irrefutable Laws of Leadership* (Nashville: Thomas Nelson, 1998), 199.

25. David L. McKenna, *Renewing Our Ministry* (Waco, TX: W Pub Group, 1986), 63.

26. Lisa Edmondson, accessed March 24, 2018, www.wishafriend.com/quotes/qid/9925/.

27. John C. Maxwell, *The Communicator's Commentary: Deuteronomy* (Waco, TX: Word Books, 1987), 151.

28. Thurston Clarke, *Pearl Harbor Ghosts* (New York: Ballantine Books, 2001), 35.

29. Presidential quotes: Glenn D. Black, *God's Revivalist*, January 7, 1982, 15.

30. Amiel Handelsman, "How to Make Peace with Your Enemies at Work and Beyond," accessed March 25, 2018, www.fastcompany.com/3029169/how-to-make-peace-with-your-enemies-at-work-and-beyond.

31. Accessed March 28, 2018, https://www.brainyquote.com/quotes/samuel_taylor_coleridge_108501.

32. Reported in *World*, July 26/August 2, 2008.

33. Cited by J. Oswald Sanders, *Spiritual Leadership* (Chicago: Moody Press, 1967), 75.

34. Reported in "Be Your Very Best at All Times," *Triangle*, Summer 2011, 7.

35. Cited by Frank Viscuso, *Step Up Your Teamwork* (Tulsa, OK: Fire Engineering Books, 2015), 148.

36. John C. Maxwell and Jim Dornan, *Becoming a Person of Influence* (Nashville: Thomas Nelson, 1997), 54.

CHAPTER 2—WORDS HAVE VALUE

1. Accessed May 6, 2018, www.brainyquote.com/quotes/stanislaw_jerzy_lec_125497.

2. Cork Millner, "The Buck Stops Here: Celebrity Writers Send In Their Best Words for $1," *Los Angeles Times*, accessed March 29, 2018, http://articles.latimes.com/1986-02-23/magazine/tm-10830_1_single-word.

3. "Einstein's Theory of Happiness," *AARP Bulletin*, January 2018, 54.

4. Accessed March 29, 2018, https://en.wikipedia.org/wiki/A_picture_is_worth_a_thousand_words.

5. "Thoughts That Count," *AARP The Magazine*, April/May 1994, 68.

6. Cited by Norman Vincent Peale, *Bible Power for Successful Living* (Pawling, NY: Peale Center for Christian Living, 1993), 160.

7. Martha Dunagin Saunders, "3 Words That Can Change Your Life," *Reader's Digest*, December 1994, 137.

8. Saunders, "3 Words That Can Change Your Life."

9. Cited by Hans Finzel, *The Top Ten Mistakes Leaders Make* (Wheaton, IL: Victor Books, 1994), 118.

10. Accessed March 31, 2018, www.brainyquote.com/quotes/plato_109439.

11. Cited by Michael Gerson, "Obama's Cool Is Leaving More People Cold," *Washington Post*, August 4, 2010, accessed April 3, 2018, www.washingtonpost.com/wp-dyn/content/article/2010/08/03/AR2010080304664.html.

12. Jo Anne Lyon, "Affirmation Is a Choice," *Light from the Word*, February 29, 1996.

13. Accessed March 31, 2018, https://quoteinvestigator.com/2014/04/06/they-feel/.

14. Accessed April 3, 2018, http://vasthead.com/Radio/rohn.html.

15. Dr. Seuss, *Horton Hatches the Egg*, accessed April 19, 2018, www.goodreads.com/quotes/44212
-i-meant-what-i-said-and-i-said-what-i.

16. Fred Smith, *Learning to Lead* (Dallas: Word Publishing, 1986), 168.

17. Accessed April 3, 2018, www.nps.gov/nr/travel/cultural_diversity/g_washington_carver_historic
_site.html.

18. Marlo Thomas, "The Givers: What Inspires Michael J. Fox? A Very Personal Interview," accessed
April 3, 2018, www.huffingtonpost.com/marlo-thomas/michael-j-fox-interview_b_1402876
.html.

19. Cited by John W. Kennedy, "Watch Your Mouth!" *New Man Magazine*, September/October 2001,
50.

20. Interview in *Vanity Fair*, October 1996.

21. Robert Boyd Munger, *Leading from the Heart* (Downers Grove, IL: InterVarsity Press, 1995), 92.

22. Gary L. McIntosh, "Growth Points," 1996.

23. John L. Mason, *An Enemy Called Average* (Tulsa, OK: Honor Books, 1993), 135.

24. Larry King, *How to Talk to Anyone, Anytime, Anywhere* (New York: Crown Publishers, 1994),
127-28.

25. Mary Hollingsworth, *The One Year Devotional of Joy and Laughter: 365 Inspirational Meditations
to Brighten Your Day* (Wheaton, IL: Tyndale House, 2011), July 26.

26. Accessed April 4, 2018, www.dalecarnegiewayindy.com/2011/09/26/7-success-lessons-from-dale
-carnegie/.

27. "Temperance Address," accessed April 4, 2018, www.abrahamlincolnonline.org/lincoln/speeches/
temperance.htm.

28. Matthew Sleeth, *24/6* (Carol Stream, IL: Tyndale House, 2012), 119-21.

29. Accessed April 4, 2018, www.brainyquote.com/quotes/diogenes_384521.

30. Accessed April 4, 2018, www.azquotes.com/quote/1400385.

31. John C. Maxwell and Jim Dornan, *Becoming a Person of Influence* (Nashville: Thomas Nelson,
1997), 80.

32. Cited by King, *How to Talk to Anyone*, 43.

33. Mark O. Wilson, *Filled Up, Poured Out* (Indianapolis: Wesleyan Publishing, 2012), 126.

34. Wilson, *Filled Up, Poured Out*, 127.

35. Cited by Gary L. McIntosh, "Growth Points," March 2015, 1.

36. David Augsburger, *Caring Enough to Hear and Be Heard* (Ventura, CA: Regal Books, 1982), 12.

37. Wilson, *Filled Up, Poured Out*, 126.

38. Cited by King, *How to Talk to Anyone*, 44.

CHAPTER 3—WORDS ENDURE

1. Accessed April 30, 2018, www.brainyquote.com/topics/endure.

2. Mark Batterson, *The Grave Robber* (Grand Rapids, MI: Baker Books, 2014), 81-82.

3. Accessed April 11, 2018, www.google.com/search?q=shakespeare&rlz=1C1EJFA_enUS738US73
8&oq=shakespeare&aqs=chrome..69i57j69i61l3j0l2.1934j0j7&sourceid=chrome&ie=UTF-8.

See also "List of best-selling fiction authors," accessed April 11, 2018, https://en.wikipedia.org/wiki/List_of_best-selling_fiction_authors.

4. Will Gompertz, "Why Is Shakespeare More Popular Than Ever?" *BBC News Magazine*, accessed April 10, 2018, www.bbc.com/news/magazine-36114485.

5. Gompertz, "Why Is Shakespeare More Popular Than Ever?"

6. Gompertz, "Why Is Shakespeare More Popular Than Ever?"

7. Gompertz, "Why Is Shakespeare More Popular Than Ever?"

8. Gompertz, "Why Is Shakespeare More Popular Than Ever?"

9. Heather Rodriguez, "Why Are Some Presidential Remarks More Memorable Than Others?" *Texas A&M Today,* February 19, 2018, accessed April 12, 2018, https://today.tamu.edu/2018/02/19/why-are-some-presidential-remarks-more-memorable-than-others/.

10. Jeremy Miller, "What Makes Some Slogans More Memorable Than Others?" December 19, 2017, accessed April 13, 2018, https://stickybranding.com/what-makes-some-slogans-more-memorable-than-others/.

11. Daniel 6:8 MSG.

12. Daniel 6:16 MSG.

13. Accessed April 17, 2018, www.sermonaudio.com/viewtranscript.asp?sermonid=425171518371&loc=20642.

14. Carmine Gallo, "Five Words That Will Make Your Pitch Memorable," *Forbes*, May 14, 2015, accessed April 13, 2018, www.forbes.com/sites/carminegallo/2015/05/14/five-words-that-will-make-your-pitch-instantly-memorable/#4989a1807a09.

15. Alina Tugend, "Praise Is Fleeting, but Brickbats We Recall," *New York Times*, March 23, 2012, accessed April 11, 2018, www.nytimes.com/2012/03/24/your-money/why-people-remember-negative-events-more-than-positive-ones.html.

16. Tugend, "Praise Is Fleeting, but Brickbats We Recall."

17. Tom Mullins, *The Confidence Factor* (Nashville: Nelson Books, 2006), 83-84.

18. Cited by Hans Finzel, *The Top Ten Mistakes Leaders Make* (Wheaton, IL: Victor Books, 1994), 56.

19. "Ac-Cent-Tchu-Ate the Positive," accessed April 16, 2018, https://en.wikipedia.org/wiki/Ac-Cent-Tchu-Ate_the_Positive.

20. Norman Vincent Peale, *Why Some Positive Thinkers Get Powerful Results* (Nashville: Thomas Nelson, 1986), 143-44.

21. Peale, *Why Some Positive Thinkers Get Powerful Results*, 145.

22. Accessed April 18, 2018, https://en.wikipedia.org/wiki/Mordecai_Brown.

23. Peale, *Why Some Positive Thinkers Get Powerful Results*, 148.

24. John Rampton, accessed April 16, 2018, www.entrepreneur.com/slideshow/307643#0.

25. Stephen Shainbart, "Horrible Words Stay Out There Forever," *AARP Bulletin*, March 2018, 20.

CHAPTER 4—FILTERING WORDS

1. Accessed September 20, 2011, http://brainyquote.com/quotes/authors/j/james_lane_allen.html.

2. Cited by James Gleick, "Albert Einstein," *Time*, March 29, 1999, 75.

3. Gleick, "Albert Einstein," 76.

4. "Tips for Social Media Distractions," accessed April 23, 2018, www.disability.illinois.edu/tips -social-media-distractions.

5. "Books vs. TV: How they Stack Up Against One Another," accessed April 23, 2018, www.huff ingtonpost.com/melissa-chu/books-vs-tv-how-they-stac_b_10928340.html.

6. "Books vs. TV: How they Stack Up Against One Another."

7. Accessed April 24, 2018, www.quora.com/How-do-I-exactly-filter-my-thoughts.

8. Harvey Mackay, *Swim with the Sharks* (New York: William Morrow, 1988), 268-69.

9. Accessed April 24, 2018, www.azquotes.com/quote/926563.

10. Ken Blanchard, *Mission Possible* (New York: McGraw Hill, 1999), 10.

11. Max Lucado, *He Still Moves Stones* (Dallas: Word Publishing, 1993), 90.

12. C.S. Lewis, quoted in *Student Leadership Journal*, Fall 1996, 34.

13. Cited in John C. Maxwell, *Beyond Talent* (Nashville: Thomas Nelson, 2007), 42.

14. Robert H. Schuller, *Tough Times Never Last, But Tough People Do* (Nashville: Thomas Nelson, 1983), 94.

15. Aja Frost, "Better Brainstorming: The Most Effective Way to Generate More Ideas," accessed April 25, 2018, https://zapier.com/blog/brainstorming/.

16. Frost, "Better Brainstorming."

17. Jim Rohn, accessed April 25, 2018, www.azquotes.com/quote/613241.

18. Schuller, *Tough Times Never Last*, 188-89.

19. Accessed April 25, 2018, http://edmundrice.net/our-way-into-the-future/what-is-owitf/2-un categorised-sp-786/1513-praying-during-the-week.

20. Cited in Marshall Wall, *From Where I Sit, From Where You Stand* (Bloomington, IN: AuthorHouse, 2007), 92.

21. Schuller, *Tough Times Never Last*, 190. All five of the ways some people respond to ideas are from Schuller.

22. Harvey Mackay, accessed April 25, 2018, https://quotefancy.com/quote/822534/Harvey-MacKay -Ideas-without-action-are-worthless.

23. Mark Twain, accessed April 26, 2018, www.bartleby.com/73/540.html.

24. Mackay, *Swim with the Sharks,* 226-27.

25. Larry King, *How to Talk to Anyone, Anytime, Anywhere* (New York: Crown Publishers, 1994), 78-79.

26. Benjamin Disraeli, accessed April 26, 2018, www.brainyquote.com/quotes/benjamin_disraeli _154163.

27. Beth Walker, "Talk Your Walk," *New Man*, March/April 1996, 72.

28. Alistair Cooke, *The Patient Has the Floor* (New York: Open Road Media, 2014), 12-13.

CHAPTER 5—BLESSING OTHERS

1. Accessed May 10, 2018, www.brainyquote.com/quotes/john_wooden_446989?src=t_blessings.

2. Accessed May 2, 2018, www.etymonline.com/word/bless.

3. Accessed May 2, 2018, www.lifewithoutlimbs.org/about-nick/bio/.

4. Accessed May 6, 2018, http://hourofpower.org/episode/be-the-hands-and-feet/.

5. Accessed May 10, 2018, www.brainyquote.com/quotes/henry_ward_beecher_124703.

6. "A Feat of Strength," *Have a Good Day*, November 2000.

7. Norman Vincent Peale, *Bible Power for Successful Living* (Pawling, NY: Peale Center for Christian Living, 1993), 95.

8. Accessed May 6, 2018, https://en.wikipedia.org/wiki/Mia_Hamm.

9. Marlo Thomas, *The Right Words at the Right Time* (New York: Atria Books, 2002), 149-51.

10. Sam Klomhaus, "The Five Best Female Soccer Players of All Time," accessed May 6, 2018, https://the18.com/soccer-entertainment/lists/5-best-female-soccer-players-of-all-time.

11. Kevin Myers and John Maxwell, *Home Run* (New York: Faith Words, 2014), 181.

12. Accessed May 9, 2018, www.brainyquote.com/quotes/andrew_carnegie_408624.

13. Jim Rohn, accessed May 10, 2018, www.beyondsuccess.com.au/bootcamps/emotional-intelligence/.

14. Ann Cetas, "Whispering Words," *Our Daily Bread*, March 17, 2018.

15. Bill Vossler, "How to Choose Your Feelings," *Kiwanis*, June/July, 1993, 31.

16. Vossler, "How to Choose Your Feelings," 32.

17. Vossler, "How to Choose Your Feelings," 33.

18. Vossler, "How to Choose Your Feelings."

19. Barbara Bush, *Reflections: Life After the White House* (New York: Scribner, 2003), 289-90.

20. Cited by Manny Fernandez, "Barbara Bush Is Remembered at Her Funeral for Her Wit and Tough Love," *New York Times*, April 21, 2018, accessed May 8, 2018, www.nytimes.com/2018/04/21/us/barbara-bush-funeral.html.

21. Charles Lowery, "Rhinos and Buffalo Birds," *SBC Life*, May 2005, accessed May 8, 2018, www.sbclife.net/Articles/2005/05/sla12.

22. Wayne Schmidt, *Soul Management* (Grand Rapids, MI: Zondervan, 1996), 84-85.

23. Lee Strobel, *God's Outrageous Claims* (Grand Rapids, MI: Zondervan, 1997), 121.

24. Beth Wolfensberger, "Friends and Family," *Colorado Springs Independent*, September 13, 1995, 7.

25. Ted Engstrom, *The Fine Art of Friendship* (Nashville: Thomas Nelson, 1985), 30-31.

26. Gordon MacDonald, *The Life God Blesses* (Nashville: Thomas Nelson, 1994), 1-4.

27. Eric Metaxas and Stan Guthrie, "Good News About Prayer," *Breakpoint,* accessed May 7, 2018, www.breakpoint.org/2018/05/breakpoint-good-news-about-prayer/.

28. Metaxas and Guthrie, "Good News About Prayer."

29. Metaxas and Guthrie, "Good News About Prayer."

30. Accessed May 9, 2018, https://en.wikipedia.org/wiki/William_Wilberforce.

31. Cited by Sibyl Towner, "An Examined Life," *Outcomes*, Summer 2011, 14.

32. David Benner, *The Gift of Being Yourself* (Downers Grove, IL: InterVarsity Press, 2015), 41.

33. Towner, "An Examined Life," 14.

CHAPTER 6—TRUTH TELLING

1. Accessed May 13, 2018, www.goodreads.com/quotes/1287183-truth-is-always-strong-no-matter-how-weak-it-looks.

2. Marlo Thomas, *The Right Words at the Right Time* (New York: Atria Books, 2002), 91-95.

3. *Time*, October 5, 1992, 37; cited by Stuart Briscoe, *Choices for a Lifetime* (Wheaton, IL: Tyndale House, 1995), 177.

4. David J. Ley, "6 Reasons People Lie When They Don't Need To," accessed May 14, 2018, www.psychologytoday.com/us/blog/women-who-stray/201701/6-reasons-people-lie-when-they-don-t-need.

5. "What's in a Name?" *World*, accessed May 14, 2018, https://world.wng.org/2008/05/quick _takes_1.

6. Edward Wyatt, "Author Is Kicked Out of Oprah Winfrey's Book Club," *New York Times*, January 27, 2006, accessed May 14, 2018, www.nytimes.com/2006/01/27/books/27oprah.html.

7. Cited by Cal Thomas, "Too Strong a Medicine," *Baltimore Sun*, October 4, 1994, accessed May 14, 2018, http://articles.baltimoresun.com/1994-02-04/news/1994035136_1_objective-truth -koppel-personal-testimony.

8. Susan Sumner, "The Seven Levels of Lying," *Christianity Today*, May 2011, 52-53.

9. Melissa Carver, "The Truth About Lying: Why People Lie and How to Cope," accessed May 15, 2018, https://chopra.com/articles/the-truth-about-lying-why-people-lie-and-how-to-cope.

10. Carole Spiers, "When Lying Becomes a Force of Habit," accessed May 15, 2018, https://gulfnews .com/business/analysis/when-lying-becomes-a-force-of-habit-1.1195533.

11. Mark Twain, accessed May 15, 2018, www.brainyquote.com/quotes/mark_twain_133066.

12. Ley, "6 Reasons People Lie When They Don't Need To."

13. Cited by Os Guinness, "Living in Truth," *Moody*, May/June 2000, 42.

14. Guinness, "Living in Truth."

15. Yudhijit Bhattacharjee, "Why We Lie: The Science Behind Our Deceptive Ways," *National Geographic*, accessed May 15, 2018, www.nationalgeographic.com/magazine/2017/06/lying-hoax-false -fibs-science/.

16. Bhattacharjee, "Why We Lie."

17. Bhattacharjee, "Why We Lie."

18. David McCullough, *Mornings on Horseback* (New York: Simon & Schuster, 2001), 338.

19. "Treasure Check," *World*, January 26/February 3, 2008, 16.

20. Larry King, *How to Talk to Anyone, Anytime, Anywhere* (New York: Crown Publishers, 1994), 201.

21. Accessed May 22, 2018, www.brainyquote.com/quotes/thomas_jefferson_132205.

22. Cited by John L. Mason, *An Enemy Called Average* (Tulsa, OK: Honor Books, 1993), 89.

23. Mason, *An Enemy Called Average*, 90.

24. Jay Barbree, *Neil Armstrong: A Life of Flight* (New York: St. Martin's Press, 2014), 38.

25. Eric Metaxas, "What Makes Men Great: The Eric Liddell Story," *Breakpoint*, April 1, 2013.

26. D. Stuart Briscoe, *Romans: Communicators Commentary* (Dallas: Word, 1982), 99.

27. Peggy Noonan, *When Character Was King* (New York: Viking, 2001), 82-83.

28. Leo Buscaglia, accessed May 23, 2018, www.brainyquote.com/quotes/leo_buscaglia_106299.

29. Cited by Don Shula and Ken Blanchard, *Everyone's a Coach* (New York: Harper Business, 1995), 153.

30. Shula and Blanchard, *Everyone's a Coach*, 154.

CHAPTER 7—THE POWER OF SILENCE

1. Norman Vincent Peale, accessed May 24, 2018, www.azquotes.com/quote/1055853.

2. Thomas Carlyle, accessed May 24, 2018, www.phrases.org.uk/meanings/silence-is-golden.html.

3. Epictetus, accessed May 24, 2018, www.brainyquote.com/quotes/epictetus_106298.

4. Gary D. Foster, "The Foster Letter: Religious Market Update," May 25, 2018, 1.

5. Theophilus, accessed May 26, 2018, https://en.wikipedia.org/wiki/Monastic_silence.

6. "How to Tell if You Talk Too Much," *wikiHow*, accessed May 24, 2018, www.wikihow.com/Tell-if-You-Talk-Too-Much.

7. Halle Tecco, "Why We Talk (or Don't Talk) So Much," *Huffington Post*, accessed May 24, 2018, www.huffingtonpost.com/halle-tecco/why-we-talk-or-dont-talk_b_467249.html.

8. Lydia Dishman, "The Science of Why We Talk Too Much (and How to Shut Up)," *Fast Company*, accessed May 24, 2018, www.fastcompany.com/3047285/the-science-of-why-we-talk-too-much-and-how-to-shut-up.

9. Tecco, "Why We Talk (or Don't Talk) So Much."

10. Marissa Fessenden, "Which States Have the Fastest Talker?" accessed May 26, 2018, www.smithsonianmag.com/smart-news/researchers-figured-out-which-states-talk-fastest-and-which-slowest-180958033/.

11. Cited by Tony Campolo, *Let Me Tell You a Story* (Nashville: Word Publishing, 2000), 192.

12. Mark Goulston, "How to Know if You Talk Too Much," *Harvard Business Review*, accessed May 26, 2018, https://hbr.org/2015/06/how-to-know-if-you-talk-too-much.

13. "How to Tell if You Talk Too Much."

14. Cited by Arnaud Romeo Noume, *The Key Journey to Success* (Bloomington, IN: Xlibris Corporation, 2011), 40.

15. Bobb Biehl, *Dream Energy* (USA: Quick Wisdom Publishing, 2001), 142.

16. Cited by John Maxwell, *Developing the Leaders Around You* (Nashville: Thomas Nelson, 1995), 27.

17. Harvey Mackay, *Swim with the Sharks* (New York: William Morrow, 1988), 158.

18. John L. Mason, *An Enemy Called Average* (Tulsa, OK: Honor Books, 1993), 213.

19. Doug Firebaugh, "The Skill that All Success Depends On," accessed May 26, 2018, http://passionfire.com/mlm-and-network-marketing-the-skill-that-all-success-depends-on/.

20. Accessed May 24, 2018, www.pinterest.com/pin/192599321541554490/.

21. Cited by Dishman, "The Science of Why We Talk Too Much."

22. Cited by David McNally, *Even Eagles Need a Push* (New York: Delacorte Press, 1990), 117.

23. Mitch Albom, *Have a Little Faith* (New York: Hyperion, 2009), 212.

24. Remez Sasson, "What Are the Benefits of Silencing the Mind?" accessed May 24, 2018, www.successconsciousness.com/blog/inner-peace/what-are-the-benefits-of-silencing-the-mind/.

25. The ideas in this section have been strongly influenced by Paul J. Meyer, *The Dynamics of Personal Leadership* (Waco, TX: Success Motivation Institute, 1969), notes from author's file.

26. Accessed May 26, 2018, www.brainyquote.com/quotes/james_allen_133802.

27. Norman Vincent Peale, *Why Some Positive Thinkers Get Powerful Results* (Nashville: Thomas Nelson, 1986), 62-63.

CHAPTER 8—YOUR ATTITUDE SAYS EVERYTHING

1. Tim Stafford, "Can We Talk?," *Christianity Today*, October 2, 1995, 32.

2. Mike Wise, "Pushed Beyond the Limit," *Washington Post*, August 30, 2004, accessed May 28, 2018, www.washingtonpost.com/wp-dyn/articles/A45340-2004Aug29.html?nav=rss_sports/leagues andsports/olympics/2004summer.

3. Max Lucado, *Every Day Deserves a Chance* (Nashville: Thomas Nelson, 2007), 23-24.

4. Yogi Berra, accessed May 28, 2018, www.theglobeandmail.com/news/world/yogi-berras-famous -quotes-baseball-is-90-per-cent-mental-the-other-half-is-physical/article26494911/.

5. From author's file, no other attribution available.

6. Denis Waitley, accessed May 28, 2018, www.brainyquote.com/quotes/denis_waitley_363622.

7. Denis Waitley, accessed May 28, 2018, www.azquotes.com/quote/576007.

8. Cited by George Sweeting, "A Supernatural Attitude," *Moody*, March-April 2000, 84.

9. William James, accessed May 28, 2018, www.brainyquote.com/quotes/william_james_104186.

10. Accessed May 28, 2018, https://allauthor.com/quotes/84807/.

11. Tom Mullins, *The Confidence Factor* (Nashville: Nelson Books, 2006), 165.

12. John C. Maxwell, *Your Road Map for Success* (Nashville: Thomas Nelson, 2002), 53.

13. Raymond Bottom, "Just Right," *Wesleyan Advocate,* September 1996, 6.

14. Gina Conroy, Elece Hollis, and Colleen Kenny, *Reach for Your Dreams, Graduate* (Lakeland, FL: White Stone Books, 2005), 167.

15. Edwin Markham, accessed May 28, 2018, www.goodreads.com/quotes/8703-he-drew-a-circle -that-shut-me-out--heretic.

16. Norman Vincent Peale, *Power Your Life with Positive Thinking* (Pawling, NY: Guideposts, 2013), 11-12.

17. Credit William Barclay for the nuances on the Greek terms, *The Letter to the Romans* (Philadelphia: Westminster Press, 1975), 158.

18. Larry King, *How to Talk to Anyone, Anytime, Anywhere* (New York: Crown Publishers, 1994), 105.

19. John Mason, *You Were Born an Original, Don't Die a Copy* (Grand Rapids, MI: Revell, 2011), 59.

20. Mark J. Perry, "Fortune 500 firms 1955 v. 2016," *AE Ideas*, accessed May 28, 2018, www.aei.org/ publication/fortune-500-firms-1955-v-2016-only-12-remain-thanks-to-the-creative-destruction -that-fuels-economic-prosperity/.

21. John L. Mason, *An Enemy Called Average* (Tulsa, OK: Honor Books, 1993), 127-28.

22. "To Illustrate Plus," *Leadership*, Winter 1998, 71.

23. Accessed May 28, 2018, https://en.wikiquote.org/wiki/Winston_Churchill.

24. Accessed May 28, 2018, www.goodreads.com/author/quotes/1538.Stephen_R_Covey?page=10.

25. Accessed May 28, 2018, www.wisdomtoinspire.com/t/winston-churchill/VyeUWnbmK/there-is -nothing-wrong-with-change-if-it-is-in-the-right-direction.

26. Accessed May 28, 2018, https://teachhoops.com/great-quotes-for-your-basketball-team-and -players/.

27. Cited in Maxwell, *Your Road Map for Success*, 71.

28. Maxwell, *Your Road Map for Success*.

29. Robert Frost, "The Road Not Taken," accessed May 28, 2018, www.poetryfoundation.org/poems/44272/the-road-not-taken.

30. E. James Rohn, *The Five Major Pieces to the Life Puzzle* (Dallas, TX: Great Impressions Printing & Graphics, 1991), 73.

31. *The Pastor's Story File*, September 1992, 8.

32. Stephen R. Covey, "Body, Mind, Heart," *Priorities*, November/December 2000, 31.

33. Accessed May 28, 2018, www.brainyquote.com/quotes/theodore_roosevelt_403358.

34. Covey, "Body, Mind, Heart."

CHAPTER 9–POSITIVE WORD POWER

1. Brian Tracy, accessed June 2, 2018, www.azquotes.com/quote/798650.

2. Larry Chang, ed., *Wisdom for the Soul* (Washington, DC: Gnosophia Publishers, 2006), 373.

3. Marlo Thomas, *The Right Words at the Right Time* (New York: Atria Books, 2002), 376-78.

4. Viktor E. Frankl, *Man's Search for Meaning* (Boston: Beacon Press, 2006), 66.

5. Earl Nightingale, from author's file, no other attribution available.

6. Cited in Earle Wilson, *Holy and Human* (Indianapolis: Wesleyan Publishing House, 2008), 91-92.

7. Les Parrott III, "Making the Right Choice," *Rev!*, July/August 2000, 33.

8. Francie Baltazar-Schwartz, accessed May 30, 2018, http://blasiegroup.sas.upenn.edu/strzalka/attitude.html.

9. Joni Eareckson Tada, "Affirming Others," accessed May 31, 2018, https://justbetweenus.org/health/relationship-health/encouraging-and-affirming-others/.

10. Proverbs 12:25 NLT.

11. Don Shula and Ken Blanchard, *Everyone's a Coach* (New York: Harper Business, 1995), 129.

12. Accessed May 31, 2018, www.brainyquote.com/quotes/samuel_goldwyn_150932.

13. "Bandleader Skitch Henderson Dies at 87," *Today*, accessed May 31, 2018, www.today.com/popculture/bandleader-skitch-henderson-dies-87-wbna9892634.

14. Cited in John Maxwell and Jim Dornan, *Becoming a Person of Influence* (Nashville: Thomas Nelson, 1997), 166.

15. Cited by Harold Ivan Smith, *Grieving the Death of a Friend* (Minneapolis: Augsburg Books, 1996), 46.

16. Adapted from a list cited by blogger Nate Claiborne, who referred to Sam Crabtree's book, *Practicing Affirmation* (Wheaton, IL: Crossway Books, 2011).

17. Marlo Thomas, *The Right Words at the Right Time* (New York: Atria Books, 2002), 307-8.

18. J. Oswald Sanders, *Spiritual Leadership* (Chicago: Moody Press, 1967), 91.

19. Sanders, *Spiritual Leadership*.

20. Sanders, *Spiritual Leadership*, 92.

21. Accessed June 1, 2018, https://burg.com/2010/08/tact-the-language-of-strength/.

22. Cited by Norman Vincent Peale, *In God We Trust* (Pawling, NY: Peale Center for Christian Living, 1994), 30.

23. Peale, *In God We Trust*, 31.

24. Mark O. Wilson, *Filled Up, Poured Out* (Indianapolis: Wesleyan Publishing House, 2012), 128.

25. Accessed June 1, 2018, www.goodreads.com/author/quotes/59853.Henry_Drummond.

26. Jim Miller, "Forgiving: Easier Said Than Done," *Wesleyan Advocate*, December 1998, 29.

27. Corrie ten Boom, *Tramp for the Lord* (Old Tappan, NJ: Fleming H. Revell, 1974), 180.

28. John L. Mason, *An Enemy Called Average* (Tulsa, OK: Honor Books, 1993), 132.

29. Tim Madigan, *I'm Proud of You: My Friendship with Fred Rogers* (Los Angeles: Ubuntu Press, 2012), 3-4.

CHAPTER 10—NEGATIVE WORD POWER

1. Cited by Elizabeth Irvin Ross, *Write Now* (New York: Barnes & Noble Books, 1993), 62.

2. David Aikman, *A Man of Faith: The Spiritual Journey of George W. Bush* (Nashville: W Publishing Group, 2004), 42.

3. Cited by Karl Keating, "Appealing and Appalling," accessed June 6, 2018, www.catholic.com/magazine/online-edition/appealing-and-appalling.

4. Harvey Mackay, *Swim with the Sharks* (New York: William Morrow, 1988), 257-58.

5. Robert McGarvey, "Psst…did you hear…," *Kiwanis*, June/July 1995, 26.

6. McGarvey, "Psst…did you hear…."

7. Proverbs 18:8.

8. Adapted from WinePress Publishing, accessed June 4, 2018, https://beautifulgrace2008.blogspot.com/2007/12/recipe-for-gossip.html.

9. Adapted from Whitney Hopler, "5 Ways to Stop Gossip in Its Tracks," accessed June 4, 2018, www.crosswalk.com/faith/women/5-ways-to-stop-gossip-in-its-tracks.html.

10. Mother Theresa, compiled by Jaya Chaliha and Edward Le Joly, *The Joy in Loving* (India: Penguin Books, 1996), 406.

11. Nicola Davies, "The Argumentative Personality," accessed June 6, 2018, https://healthpsychologyconsultancy.wordpress.com/2013/08/21/the-argumentative-personality/.

12. Tony Campolo, *Let Me Tell You a Story* (Nashville: Word Publishing, 2000), 86.

13. John Paul Carinci, *Awesome Success Principles and Quotations* (Bloomington, IN: AuthorHouse, 2014), Kindle edition.

14. Neel Burton, "How to Deal With Insults and Put-downs," *Psychology Today*, accessed June 4, 2018, www.psychologytoday.com/us/blog/hide-and-seek/201302/how-deal-insults-and-put-downs.

15. Accessed June 6, 2018, https://literarydevices.net/innuendo/.

16. Johnathan Kana, "Taking the Sting Out," *Light from the Word*, March-May 2017, April 8.

17. Alluded to by J.W. Douglas in *The Pacific*, vol. 50, 1901, 10, accessed June 6, 2018, https://books.google.com/books?id=OzJFAAAAYAAJ&dq=man+who+promised+Lincoln%27s+son+he+would+give+him+a+charm&source=gbs_navlinks_s.

18. George E. LaMore Jr., "Of Cuss," *Christian Herald*, February 1969, 45.

19. Kegan Mosier, "5 Ways to Tame Your Tongue," accessed June 6, 2018, www.christiancounselingco.com/5-ways-to-tame-your-tongue/.

20. Adapted from Mosier, "5 Ways to Tame Your Tongue."

21. LaMore Jr., "Of Cuss," 31.

22. LaMore Jr., "Of Cuss."

23. Cited by John W. Kennedy, "Watch Your Mouth!" *New Man*, September/October 2001, 50.

24. From author's file, no other attribution available.

25. Anya Bateman, "I'm Sick of the 'F' Word," *Reader's Digest*, vol. 134, 1989, 96.

26. Kennedy, "Watch Your Mouth," 52.

27. Kennedy, "Watch Your Mouth," 50.

28. Kennedy, "Watch Your Mouth," 53.

29. Bateman, "I'm Sick of the 'F' Word," 97.

30. Bateman, "I'm Sick of the 'F' Word," 98.

THE POWER OF YOUR ATTITUDE

As much as you try, sometimes you just can't change your circumstances—and never the actions of others. But you do have the power to choose how your attitude affects your outlook on your day and those you influence in your life.

Join Stan Toler as he shares the *what, why,* and *how* behind the transformation you desire. With this book, you'll...

- release the thoughts and habits that keep you from experiencing joy on a daily basis
- learn the seven choices you can make to get out of a rut and into greater success
- implement a plan to improve your outlook in three vital areas and conquer negativity

Having lost his father in an industrial accident as a boy, Toler knows about coping with unexpected tragedies and harsh realities. He will gently guide you through the internal processes that can positively change any life—including yours.

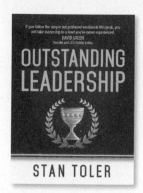

OUTSTANDING LEADERSHIP

What makes a leader stand out? What are the keys to truly making a difference? And how can you become the influencer you were created to be? With more than 40 years of leadership experience, Stan Toler knows what it takes to empower people to reach organizational and personal goals. He cuts through the mystery and confusion and provides clear guidelines to help you accomplish vital leadership tasks, including...

- defining your vision, developing your plan, and communicating clearly to help people buy in to your shared goal
- overcoming common leadership challenges to create a culture of success
- building strong relationships and effective teams that make working hard worthwhile

You'll find all the tools, tips, and practical guidance you need to help individuals and groups reach their highest potential and fulfill their God-given purpose.

STAN TOLER

Minute
Motivators
—o—
for
Leaders

*Quick Inspiration for the
Time of Your Life*

MINUTE MOTIVATORS
FOR LEADERS

You are a leader—people look to you to be an example, offer direction, and provide inspiration. But with so much to do, how can you keep fresh, focused, and excited about your opportunity to make a difference in people's lives? Stan Toler provides inspirational quotes, one-page gems of wisdom, and memorable taglines to fuel your passion and clarify your vision. You'll find plenty of helpful reminders that...

- Leaders are in the people business. As a leader, your primary function is not to buy, sell, or ply a trade. It is to understand and work with people.

- Bureaucrats run institutions. Leaders lead people. You can make the difference.

- Leadership is a team sport. Do more than direct individuals—build a team.

This treasure of tried-and-true principles will be your on-the-go source for the motivation and encouragement you need to be the effective leader you were created to be.

MINUTE MOTIVATORS FOR WOMEN
STAN TOLER AND LINDA TOLER

Whether you pick up this book first thing in the morning or when you're winding down at bedtime, you'll be inspired and encouraged over and over again!

Author Stan Toler and his wife, Linda, share thought-provoking quotes and beautiful words of hope within these pages. Each chapter will draw your attention to a single attribute every godly woman wants to cultivate in her life, such as patience, wisdom, persistence, courage, and gratitude.

Bite-size portions of inspiration make this the perfect devotional for, well, anytime—especially those days when you feel like you can never get ahead. Recharge in the middle of a hectic schedule or end your day with a much-needed reminder that God has every aspect of your life under control.